HOW TRUMP HAPPENED

HOW TRUMP HAPPENED

A System Shock Decades in the Making

Steven E. Schier and Todd E. Eberly

ROWMAN & LITTLEFIELD

Lanham • Boulder • New York • London

Published by Rowman & Littlefield
An imprint of The Rowman & Littlefield Publishing Group, Inc.
4501 Forbes Boulevard, Suite 200, Lanham, Maryland 20706
www.rowman.com

6 Tinworth Street, London SE11 5AL, United Kingdom

British Library Cataloguing in Publication Information Available

Library of Congress Cataloging-in-Publication Data

Names: Schier, Steven E., author. | Eberly, Todd E., author.
Title: How Trump happened : a system shock decades in the making / Steven E. Schier
and Todd E. Eberly.
Description: Lanham, Maryland : Rowman & Littlefield, [2020] | Includes bibliographical
references and index. | Summary: "Racism. Sexism. Russian interference. A few thousand
votes in key swing states. There are no shortage of explanations for the stunning 2016
election of Donald Trump. In How Trump Happened, political experts Steven Schier
and Todd Eberly step back to trace the factors driving his election, arguing that Trump's
victory was decades in the making. As Americans prepare once again to cast their
presidential ballots, How Trump Happened will be indispensable reading for anyone
seeking to understand the current political landscape unprecedented 2016 election and
Trump presidency" — Provided by publisher.
Identifiers: LCCN 2019045627 (print) | LCCN 2019045628 (ebook) | ISBN
9781538122044 (cloth) | ISBN 9781538122051 (epub)
Subjects: LCSH: Trump, Donald, 1946– | Presidents—United States—Election—2016.
| Political culture—United States. | Right and left (Political science)—United States. |
Polarization (Social sciences)—United States. | Divided government—United States.
| United States—Politics and government—1945–1989. | United States—Politics and
government—1989– | United States—Social conditions—1945–
Classification: LCC E911 .S35 2020 (print) | LCC E911 (ebook) | DDC
973.933092—dc23
LC record available at https://lccn.loc.gov/2019045627
LC ebook record available at https://lccn.loc.gov/2019045628

♾™ The paper used in this publication meets the minimum requirements
of American National Standard for Information Sciences—Permanence of
Paper for Printed Library Materials, ANSI/NISO Z39.48-1992.

For the women in my life: Mary, Anna, and Teresa

—Steven Schier

For my wife, Christina, who tolerates and supports my obsession with the very thing that she dislikes most—contemporary American politics. Thank you!

—Todd Eberly

CONTENTS

1

OUR ANGRY POLITICS

How did a billionaire and reality TV star with no political experience and a campaign in a seeming state of constant chaos defeat one of the most experienced, well-known, and well-funded political dynasties in America (two dynasties if you include his defeat of Jeb Bush in the GOP primary)? Though there is no shortage of theories, including racism, sexism, and Russian interference, it is worth considering the possibility that the outcome of the election was predictable. Though stunning, the 2016 election of Donald Trump to the presidency was decades in the making.

Three trends since the 1960s created the conditions for his triumph. First, a growing popular discontent with government, long evident in public opinion surveys, created a widespread distrust of established leaders and institutions. Second, America underwent the rise of "professional government." Governing professionals are an elite built on merit through occupational accomplishment. They now dominate interest groups, the bureaucracy, courts, institutional presidency, and Congress. Many government professionals perceive little need to mobilize the public in the way parties did in previous eras. This has furthered the sense of disconnect among the public and created a self-reinforcing chain. Third, political parties and governing institutions are now polarized around rival teams of ideological, partisan elites. Democrats are increasingly uniformly progressive and Republicans uniformly conservative. The intense battles between these polarized teams often result in government gridlock.

The three trends are mutually reinforcing. Distant government professionals help to fuel popular discontent. Polarized political warfare among political activists and governmental officials and the gridlock it produces spurs popular disgust with the squabbling and empowers professional governmental employees when elected officials create polarized paralysis.

Recent decades have witnessed a collapse in confidence, or trust, in government and the rise of negative partisanship driven not by loyalty to party but rather opposition to the other party. A driving force behind both is voter anger. That anger produces an environment ripe for populist candidates as well as recurrent populist uprisings among the electorate. As such, it's important to establish what each means.

POPULAR DISCONTENT AND PROFESSIONAL GOVERNMENT

Since the 1960s, trust in government has declined and remained at low levels. Along with declining party identification, low trust is an indicator of greater public disaffection with the political system. A widely studied measure of trust comes from the University of Michigan's National Election Studies (NES). Since 1964, the NES has computed a "Trust Index" of responses to four questions: (1) How much of the time do you think you can trust the government in Washington to do what is right—just about always, most of the time, or only some of the time? (2) Do you think that people in government waste a lot of the money we pay in taxes, waste some of it, or don't waste very much of it? (3) Would you say that government is pretty much run by a few big interests looking out for themselves or that it is run for the benefit of all the people? (4) Do you think that quite a few of the people running the government are crooked, not very many are, or do you think hardly any of them are crooked?

The Trust Index score ranges from 0–100. A low score indicates a lack of trust while a higher score is indicative of greater public trust in government. In 1966 the Trust Index score was 61, but within a decade it fell to 30. Though there were occasional upticks in the score, it hovered near 30 for most of the 1970s until 2008 before falling to 17 in 2016.

What caused the collapse of the Trust Index score? Researchers have identified many possible explanations: economic difficulties, crime rates, child poverty, citizens' evaluations of incumbents and institutions, political scandals and negative media coverage of politics. The Trust Index fell during decades that witnessed a divisive Vietnam War, a civil rights revolution, the impeachment of two presidents, a presidential resignation and pardon, severe recessions and stagflation, periods of high unemployment, and the rise of polarized politics.

Additionally, the rise of more "professionalism" among governing elites has contributed to a dissatisfied and unhappy public. Those in various professional occupations now dominate American government due to the rise in education levels since the 1950s and the need for informed policy experts to carry out the ever-growing responsibilities of government. Even at the state level, there has been an increase in the number of professional legislatures since the 1960s. Governing professionals are an elite built on merit through occupational accomplishment. They now populate interest groups, the bureaucracy, courts, the institutional presidency, and Congress.

Many governing professionals perceive little need to mobilize the public broadly the way political parties did in previous eras. Three examples illustrate this. First, candidates now narrowly target their appeals to likely voters. Second, unelected judges increasingly engage in policymaking behavior previously the province of elected legislatures. Third, the great growth in professional interest group activity since 1970 has produced a proliferation of elite advocacy strategies. In an era of professional advocacy, policymaking need not involve the successful channeling of mass preferences.

Changing behavior in national institutions transformed governance as well. Congressional incumbents' electoral security improved considerably during the 1960s and 1970s and that security contributed to legislative professionalism. In 1960, the total individual staff for Representatives was 2,444 or an average of nearly 6 staff members per legislator. Comparable increases occurred in staff for Senators. Committee and subcommittee staff increased as well. Total committee staff numbered 394 in 1960 and grew to over 1,200 by 2005. By 1974 the number of staff had more than doubled to 5,109 or 12 staff members per legislator. In the Senate, committee staff rose from 433 in 1960 to 883 in 2005.

The total Congressional workforce, including support resources such as the Congressional Research Service and the Congressional Budget Office, grew dramatically as well during this period. As a result of this growth, each Representative and Senator essentially runs a small business and relies on their staff to manage day-to-day responsibilities, analyze and draft legislation, help solve constituent problems, and work toward reelection.

For all the changes that took place in Congress there was a far greater transformation of the executive branch. The president sits atop an ever-thickening executive branch that reaches far beyond the president's oval office operation to the Executive Office of the President (EOP), a series of presidential bureaucracies employing about four thousand people as well as roughly 2.5 million civilian employees who manage or staff the myriad federal agencies tasked with implementing federal laws and policies.

Closest to the president is the White House Office that includes top staff in charge of media relations, Congressional relations, policy planning and executive branch appointments. The president's Office of Management and Budget (OMB) employs about 529 people who perform crucial functions such as composing the annual budget proposal, improving management in the executive branch, recommending vetoes and "legislative clearance"—determining which policy ideas from the executive branch go to Congress as presidential proposals.

Another major EOP organization is the National Security Council that meets regularly to assess and manage security threats to the nation. Its statutory members include the president, vice president, and the secretaries of the departments of State, Defense, and Energy, along with other officials invited by the president. The head of the council's staff, the National Security Adviser, is a top presidential aide who also attends all meetings of the council.

Beyond the EOP lie the fifteen departments of the president's cabinet. The Department of Health and Human Services, with its administration of the massive Social Security (retirement income), Medicare (retiree health care), and Medicaid (health care for the poor), has the largest budget. The Department of Defense has the largest number of employees. The departments of Justice and Treasury deal with law enforcement and financial management respectively and are two of the oldest departments. The other departments have authority over areas of domestic policy: Veterans Affairs, Transportation, Housing and Urban Development, Commerce, Education, Energy, Homeland Security, Agriculture, and Interior.

All told, the cabinet departments employ about two million civilian employees. Most do not work in Washington, DC, but in regional field offices spread throughout the United States. In the early and middle part of the twentieth century, many federal jobs were clerical and required few specialized skills. The federal government has retained some lower-skill jobs, but many positions now require high educational attainment and specialized training.

The changes that took place were not limited to those in government as demonstrated by the dramatic expansion in the number of Washington interest groups since 1960. The growth of interest groups since 1960 is recorded in the *Encyclopedia of Associations*. The number of interest groups, or associations grew from fewer than five thousand to slightly more than twenty-five thousand between 1955 and 2012.

One reason for their growing activities in Washington was the growth of government itself. In the 1960s, the "Great Society" programs of President Lyndon Johnson expanded government in a variety of ways. Medicare and Medicaid, passed in 1965, provided government health insurance for the elderly and poor. Congress increased Social Security benefits several times between 1960 and 1980. Under Johnson's successor, Richard

Nixon, new regulatory laws and new implementing agencies, such as the Environmental Protection Agency and Occupational Safety and Health Administration, further expanded the national government's reach. New cabinet departments, like Housing and Urban Development, Education, and Energy arose to implement new domestic programs.

The number of annual pages in the *Federal Register*, the publication forum for new regulations, expanded from 14,479 in 1960 to 87,012 in 1980. Accompanying new laws, bureaucracies and regulations were groups seeking to shape the direction of governmental efforts. Professional associations—a diverse assemblage ranging from the National Science Teachers Association to the American Chiropractic Association—were at the forefront of this trend.

Today, a dizzying variety of advocacy organizations populates Washington, placing incessant demands upon government. Approximately six hundred American corporations pursue influence there, alongside two thousand trade associations engaged in similar activities. Trade associations—ranging from the Automobile Manufacturers Association to the National Association of Theatre Owners and Association for Dressings and Sauces (the condiment-making crowd)—are groups of businesses engaged in the same area of commerce who lobby for their common interests. Dozens of unions also have a permanent Washington presence, representing crafts (such as the United Brotherhood of Carpenters), industry (United Mine Workers), and in broad federations (American Federation of Labor—Congress of Industrial Organizations). In addition, hundreds of organizations pursue postmaterial agendas (such as the National Gay and Lesbian Task Force, the Christian Coalition, and the Sierra Club).

These thousands of organizations hire a wide variety of professionals to further their advocacy efforts. Among the professions that have thrived in DC's interest group world are lawyers, public relations specialists, policy researchers and analysts, and lobbyists. All these occupations have professional associations with governing boards, announced professional standards, education and training sessions, and membership programs. In addition to hiring professionals, many interest groups contract the services of specialized firms of professionals. In DC, professional lobbying firms employ about 150 former Members of Congress to push clients' agendas before government. Many Washington law firms employ lawyers as lobbyists for clients. Public and governmental relations firms conduct lobbying and media campaigns on behalf of their clients.

A big, entrenched world of influence grew in response to a larger national government. Its demands have further maintained and expanded the reach of that government. America's vast interest group establishment feeds a perception of self-dealing, corruption, and a rampant pursuit of self-interest.

Increasingly professional government and interest advocacy have made federal policymaking a process with far more complex interactions than in 1960. This has sorely taxed the operation of a legislature, executive, and judiciary operating under our separation of powers system. Coordination and compromise are essential to the successful operation of separate institutions that must share powers. Thicker government in our national institutions, coupled with a densely populated, active, and professional interest group world escalates the coordination and information costs of governing. The scale and complexity of information now generated in the process of governing is vastly larger than a half decade ago. A big complicating element is the diversifying professional competencies among governmental players and the surrounding interest group advocates. Diverse competencies contribute to divergent agendas among a large group of individuals and organizations affected by government actions.

One outcome of all this diversity and complexity is policy stasis. A landmark study of interest groups in Washington found that their large and diverse presence leads to durable policy stability. Lobbying in Washington is geared not toward the creation of new programs, but rather the adjustment or maintenance of existing programs. As a result, it is the defenders of the status quo who usually prevail in DC.[1]

The sole exception to stasis is when the president actively pushes for policy change, but this does not happen often. Presidents have crowded domestic and foreign agendas, many distractions, and limited time in office. They are far more likely to prevail when they are popular and then only with a few issues to which they devote inordinate time and energy. That means stasis rules most of the time.

POLARIZATION

Polarization and partisanship are central features of contemporary politics and promote popular discontent and voter anger and are covered in greater detail in the following chapter but require a brief introduction here. As the Democratic and Republican parties diverged ideologically and became more internally cohesive after the late 1960s, Congressional rules and procedures were reformed to give greater power to the majority party and to make it easier to ignore or sideline the minority party.

In the Senate, where unlimited debate has long been a hallmark of the institution, the number of votes needed to end a filibuster was lowered from two-thirds (sixty-seven) to three-fifths (sixty) in 1975. During the same time, the Speaker of the House gained control of the House Rules Committee. This meant the Speaker gained control of the terms of debate for legislation on the House floor. Increasingly, rules were imposed that severely restricted or even eliminated any opportunity to amend or even debate legislation.

There was a tenfold increase in the share of major legislation subject to restrictive rules between the 89th Congress in 1966 and the 110th in 2008. During the same period, the number of days in session and the number of committee and subcommittee meetings fell dramatically. Legislation was increasingly subject to change by party leadership outside the committee process. All these changes worked to minimize the influence and input of minority party members.

Relegated to the sidelines, minority party members sought ways to obstruct the process. Minority Republicans took advantage of recorded votes and the presence of television cameras in the House and Senate chambers by forcing Democrats in competitive districts to cast votes against politically popular amendments. In the Senate, minority Republicans and then minority Democrats made increasing use of the filibuster to derail legislation.[2]

These tactics, coupled with an ongoing decline of the number of members who bridged the ideological divide between the two parties, served to bolster a sense of mistrust and even animosity between the parties. This tendency is enhanced as the positions of the two parties become more divergent.[3] The cause of this comes down to the consequences of loss. If the parties hold deep ideological differences they are likely to pursue fundamentally different policies. As such, the price of losing a legislative battle would be quite high.

The increasingly competitive nature of politics worked to diminish the opportunity for compromise. Why does increased competition decrease the likelihood of compromise? Consider the motivations of the minority party under a system where the majority party dominates and there is little chance of the minority party gaining control of the levers of government. Under such a system, the minority party gains little from obstruction and instead risks being shut out by the majority party. If, however, the minority party works to find common ground and acts as a constructive partner then there is at least the chance that some of their priorities may be given voice. Under a competitive system where the minority knows that it may regain control as early as the next election there is less motivation to seek common ground.

Instead, the minority seeks to delay and obstruct the majority party. In return, the majority party works to sideline the minority party. Why the lack of compromise? Neither side wants voters to view the other side as effective or legitimate. The result is often policy stasis. Our present system is defined by ever rising levels of professionalization, polarization, and electoral competition. Individually these features tend to result in policy stasis. Collectively they frustrate the voters as much as they frustrate the system and the level of voter frustration has become more obvious in our elections.

THE POPULIST RESPONSE

The size and complexity of national government and the multiplicity of demands brought before it require both liberals and conservatives to harness it for their ends rather than dramatically restructure or downsize it. The dream of the early professionalizers, the progressives—that national government becomes a continuing exercise in policy progress through innovation—is America's twenty-first century reality.

So why doesn't the public trust it? Why the popular discontent? Professional national government has brought us complexity, diversity, and stasis. Complexity makes it difficult for many in the public to understand just what national government is up to. Diversity ensures endless dispute about every public issue as groups ceaselessly jostle for advantage. Stasis signals that usually nothing much changes, that government is unresponsive in the face of many citizens' individual needs, and the public dislikes the pointless political conflict they believe to be rampant in American politics today.[4] The central irony here is that national politics is highly organized in a way to represent more interests than ever before. Its huge scale, however, makes it all seem a confusing blur to many citizens.

Many in the public are afraid of the self-dealing involved in the arcane negotiations among governing professionals. Policy talk, after all, is not normal discourse for most citizens. Combine this with a series of governmental failures and scandals since the 1960s and you have enduring public resistance to professional government. Whenever national difficulties mount, popular anger focuses on professional governing elites. Contrary to accepted opinion with regard to the current era, these populist uprisings are in fact an established aspect of the current American political system. We have a system not marked by unpredictability, but rather by an era in which the elections of 1974, 1980, 1994, 2006, 2010, 2016, and 2018—in which popular discontent led to significant electoral shifts—are recurrent features of a larger electoral pattern. Governmental failures spur popular uprisings.

In 1974 it was Nixon's impeachment and a deepening recession; in 1980 it was stagflation and American hostages in Iran; 1994 witnessed hostility to fiscal deficits, expanding government, and scandals in Congress; in 2006 concerns over the Iraq war, a botched response to Hurricane Katrina, and Congressional corruption drove voters to the polls; in 2010 reaction to an expansive federal healthcare law and record federal spending, debt and deficits sparked the Tea Party Movement; in 2016 economic uncertainty and record low levels of trust in government elected a political outsider with no governing experience; and, in 2018 an unpopular tax reform bill and the rollback of environmental regulations bolstered a sense of a government working more for the wealthy and corporate interests. It remains to be seen how the public will react to impeachment proceedings in response to President Trump's July 2019 phone call with Ukrainian President Volodymyr Zelensky in which Trump asked Zelensky to work with the US Attorney General as well as Trump's personal attorney to investigate unsubstantiated allegations of wrongdoing by a potential political rival.

In 1974, 2006, and 2018 it was the Democrats who benefited from populist anger and in 1980, 1994, 2010, and 2016 it was the Republicans. It is important to understand the populism is not relegated to a single end of the ideological spectrum but rather appears at both ends. Populism can best be understood as a movement that views ordinary people as a noble group organized against self-serving and undemocratic elite opponents. Populism seeks to rally working- and middle-class voters against those elite interests. Unlike other political philosophies, populism is less about offering a pro-active agenda of policies and is instead focused on mobilizing the public in reaction against the status quo and politics as usual.

Such mobilization is more readily accomplished if trust in government is low. On the left, populist ire tends to focus on powerful and entrenched interests at the top such as corporations and governmental entities that support them. On the right, populist anger focuses on those at the top, but also those at the bottom, often viewing the middle and working class as being forgotten by a system that favors those at the top as well as many "undeserving" groups at the bottom such as the poor, racial or ethnic minorities, and immigrants.[5]

Recent years have witnessed multiple examples of populist uprisings in the United States and around the world. In nearly all cases, the populist surges were built upon the mobilization of disenchanted and angry voters, pushing back against the political establishment. Two movements demonstrate rather well the overlaps as well as distinctions between left-wing and right-wing populism. The Tea Party movement of 2009 began in response to the expansive spending and regulatory policies of the Obama administration. Surveys showed that Tea Party members tended to be white, older, and angry and usually voted Republican. Tea Party members were motivated by opposition to President Obama's healthcare reform bill, what they viewed as excessive spending by a government that did not represent the people, and economic anxiety.[6] Most members viewed a reduction in the size and influence of the federal government as their primary goal. The Tea Party movement helped deliver the House of Representatives to Republicans in the 2010 midterm elections and there is considerable overlap between those who supported the Tea Party movement and those who supported Trump in 2016.

The Occupy Wall Street movement emerged in late 2011 and quickly spread to major cities throughout the United States. Though more difficult to survey, interviews with Occupy Wall Street protesters revealed that most viewed the wealthy and corporate interests as serious threats to American prosperity. Protesters believed in a more expansive role for government in the taxation of wealth and the regulation of business. The vast majority supported the idea of free health care and forgiveness of all student debt.[7] Though the Occupy Wall Street movement and protests faded away by the end of 2012, Bernie Sanders embraced much of the movement's agenda in his 2016 and 2020 quests for the Democratic nomination for president.

Collectively, a decade that featured periods of high unemployment, low economic growth, rising levels of personal debt, and stagnant wage growth contributed to low public esteem of government, banks, and industry and greater popular distrust, discontent, and anger. This combination made the Bernie Sanders and Donald Trump candidacies viable. On the left there was a growing sense that large corporations and monied interests were able to use their influence to manipulate government and on the right there was a belief that big government cared more about special interest than it did average citizens. It was an environment tailored for the populist messaging of Sanders and Trump.

Bernie Sanders and Donald Trump were hardly the first politicians to harness and ride a wave of populism. Alabama Governor George Wallace, a well-known segregationist, sought the Democratic nomination for president in 1964, 1972, and 1976. In 1964 Wallace packaged his anti–civil rights message with attacks on a liberal press and distant Washington establishment. Wallace delivered fiery speeches at his rallies and it connected with and motivated the audience. Wallace often held rallies in areas where he knew he would attract protesters and demonstrators. These demonstrators often clashed with police and Wallace used the image of unruly protestors to convey to his supporters that such people were dangerous.

In 1972 Wallace repackaged his anti–civil rights rhetoric of prior campaigns with messaging targeting elites and "big government." At rallies Wallace would tell the crowd that the government was run by elite liberals who had lost touch with the "little people." Though Wallace had publicly disavowed his segregationist past, his rallies often played out much the same as they did in 1964. Crowds often sang "Dixie" and the Confederate Battle Flag was ubiquitous. Wallace would use the presence of protestors to convince his supporters of the importance of his fight. Wallace secured significant early primary wins only to have his candidacy cut short by an assassination attempt.

In 1992, billionaire Ross Perot campaigned for the presidency by railing against the Washington, DC, establishment. He described the nation's capital as a "town filled with sound bites, shell games, handlers, media stuntmen who posture, create images, talk, shoot off Roman candles, but don't ever accomplish anything." Despite an erratic campaign in which Perot withdrew, all but endorsed the Democrat, reentered the race, and claimed that Republicans had tried to sabotage his daughter's wedding, Perot went on to win 19 percent of the popular vote. Perot's vote total is clear evidence of a significant group of disaffected voters ready to shake up the system.[8] Though Perot hit upon many of the populist themes raised by Wallace, Perot did not tap into or exploit racial resentment as Wallace had. As an interesting side note, in the months prior to Perot's death in the summer of 2019, his son wrote two checks of the maximum legal limit to Trump's 2020 reelection.

Two years after the Perot insurgency, Republicans nationalized the 1994 midterm elections as a referendum on a corrupt Congress marred by scandal. Democrats made effective use of populist rhetoric in 2006 when they ran on a promise to "drain the swamp" in Washington—the same promise made by Donald Trump in 2016. Donald Trump's victory (and the strength of Senator Bernie Sanders in the Democratic primary) were just the most recent manifestation of these populist uprisings driven by rising levels of voter anger with the political system. An Associated Press poll released in April 2016 found that nearly 80 percent of American adults were dissatisfied or angry with the federal government. Though few predicted that Donald Trump would win the Republican nomination, let alone the presidency, the signs of a victory like his were there for years.

Like Wallace, Trump used his rallies to fire up his supporters. Trump often attracted protestors and Trump would call them out and even encourage his supporters in the audience to throw the protesters out. At one point Trump promised to pay the legal fees should one of his supporters punch a protester. Trump railed against liberals, the Washington establishment, and the press. And Trump painted a distorted picture of an America riven by crime and overrun by illegal immigrants. Trump made frequent references linking illegal immigration to the violent international criminal gang MS-13. Multiple studies conducted before and following the election found that racial resentment played a key role in Trump's victory. In one study, racism was a greater predictor of support for Trump than was economic anxiety, ideology, or partisanship. This had not been the case for prior Republican nominees.[9]

Exit polling data support the populist uprising explanation for Mr. Trump's victory. On Election Day 2016, fully 69 percent of voters were either dissatisfied with or angry at government; Mr. Trump won 58 percent of them. A plurality of voters, 48 percent, wanted the next president to be more conservative than Barack Obama; Mr. Trump won 83 percent of them. A clear plurality, 39 percent, said the quality that mattered most to them in a new president was that he/she can bring change; Mr. Trump won 83 percent of those voters. Fully half of all voters said government already does too much as opposed to too little, and Donald Trump won 73 percent of them.

Given her resume, Hillary Clinton had little choice but to be the establishment candidate. In the midst of that populist ire, she ran as the candidate of Mr. Obama's third term. She wrapped herself in the cloak of the Obama agenda. She did all this in a year when most voters did not want the establishment to win. Unfortunately for Clinton, she struggled to tap into the left-wing populist anger that had propelled Sanders.

Among other issues from her past, revelations surfaced that Clinton had collected nearly $700,000 as compensation for three speeches delivered to Goldman Sachs. Goldman Sachs is one of the largest investment banks in the world and was at the center of the 2007 subprime mortgage crisis and received a $10 billion investment from the federal government as part of the 2008 economic bailout initiative, the Troubled Asset Relief Program. When transcripts of the speeches were leaked late in the 2016 campaign, selective excerpts portrayed Clinton as being too cozy with the very folks that many Sanders supporters opposed.

Neither candidate was viewed as honest or likable, and most voters were not happy with the choice presented them in 2016. In a rather telling finding, fully 60 percent of voters said Mr. Trump was not qualified to be president. Yet he still managed to win 20 percent of those folks; 2016 was an election based on discontent and frustration, not qualifications and temperament.

Though Ms. Clinton and her supporters have offered myriad explanations for her defeat—from Russian interference, Wikileaks, James Comey's decision to reopen the investigation into Ms. Clinton's email server, and misogyny—exit poll data suggests that Ms. Clinton lost for many of the same reasons that prior candidates have lost. On Election Day, over two-thirds of the electorate were either dissatisfied with or angry at the federal government. Nearly two-thirds of the electorate said that the American economy was in poor shape and that the country was headed in the wrong direction. Mr. Trump carried those voters by wide margins.

The size and scope of what happened in November 2016 points not necessarily to a realignment in American politics, or to a result influenced by nefarious forces, but to a systemic and recurring reaction by an upset and frustrated electorate. It was the manifestation of years, in fact decades, of rising levels of discontent by a growing number of disaffected voters. And into the midst of that discontent entered two immensely unpopular candidates for president.

One, a former senator, a former secretary of state, a former candidate for president, the spouse of a former president, and the heir apparent to an outgoing two-term president was the embodiment of the very political establishment that populist uprisings rail against. The other candidate channeled that voter anger and offered those angry voters a conduit through which to express their frustration—and won.

THE LAYOUT OF THE BOOK

As stated in the opening pages of this work, we argue that the stunning 2016 election of Donald Trump to the presidency was decades in the making and three trends since the 1960s created the conditions for his triumph: (1) a growing popular discontent with government that produced widespread distrust of established leaders and institutions; (2) the rise of "professional government" that has furthered a sense of disconnect among the public; and (3) the rise of polarized political parties and governing institutions that often results in government gridlock. These trends reinforce each other as distant government professionals help to fuel popular discontent while polarized politics promotes gridlock and spurs popular discontent and a lack of trust. This opens the door for populist uprisings that seek "outsider" candidates who promise to end politics as usual. However, most of these candidates fail. Candidates like George Wallace, John Anderson, H. Ross Perot, and Ralph Nader fell far short of electoral success.

How did Donald Trump happen to leverage his outsider status into a 2016 electoral victory? Four factors propelled him into the White House. First, Trump's long career as a public celebrity gave him an identity and "brand" widely known to the public and which generated massive free media coverage as a candidate. Second, Trump and his campaign ably used social media to further amplify his message. Third, decades of polarized political elites, governmental professionalism, and mounting popular discontent made an "outsider" message attractive to millions of angry and discontented voters in 2016. Fourth, Trump was blessed with a political opponent, Hillary Clinton, who represented the polarized and professional governing class, the establishment, that Trump rightly saw as a target ripe for his outsider message and demeanor. We tell this story in the following chapters.

Effective political parties are essential for a sound democracy but, as detailed in chapter 2, American parties have suffered important decline since the 1960s. Party deterioration is a major contributor to the polarization, professionalism, and popular discontent chronicled in chapter 1. We reveal the lengthy trend of party unpopularity in public opinion and the growing ideological polarization of the small group of citizens who are party activists. Parties now act as fundraisers for their candidates, but that important campaign finance role contributes to their unpopularity.

"Negative partisanship" and "affective polarization" by party identifiers motivated by distaste of rival partisans are now mighty contributors to polarization. This polarization has led to a substantial perception gap among the electorate with Democrats and Republicans holding fundamentally misleading and wrong impressions of each other. Collectively, negative partisanship, affective polarization, and the perception gap create a political environment ripe for our angry politics. Trump routinely taps into each to keep Republican ire focused on Democrats at times when he has suffered setbacks or is mired in controversy.

Trump's career and exploits as a celebrity, covered in chapter 3, represent a broader trend of increasing celebrity power in national politics. We will present striking evidence of the ability of celebrities to influence contemporary opinion and draw examples from Trump's rise to illustrate his clout with many in the public. Trump's candidate and presidential communications strategies, including his effective use of "hero and villain" narratives in his speeches and tweets, reveal a new method for marshalling the resources of celebrity into a successful campaign for political office. However, his career as a celebrity with a manufactured persona did little to prepare him for the many legal and technical aspects of governing.

Trump's 2016 breakthroughs are many: (1) his unconventional campaign organization and tactics, (2) his early popularity among Republicans in opinion polls, (3) his successful nomination campaign, and (4) his general election victory. In chapter 4 we explain the broader context for these breakthroughs by noting how popular discontent, professional government, "negative partisanship," polarization and celebrity all contributed to these breakthroughs. Trump's use of money, media, and messaging, including his potent policy narratives and hero and villain themes, in tandem with those broader systemic trends, produced the shock of his election. The impeachment inquiry begun in late 2019 may represent the ultimate test of the limits of Trump's breakthrough.

Modern presidents have had many problems of "political capital"—amassing and retaining support from the public, Congress, and professional government. Trump has proven unconventional in governing as he wishes without great concern about his own political capital. His communication strategies garner him constant attention but have failed to increase his poll support despite a growing economy. Trump's Congressional relations remain unpredictable and variable, often producing tempestuous conflict with the Democratically controlled House of Representatives. There is perhaps no greater example of this than the opening of an impeachment inquiry against Trump. Chapter 5 includes a presidential narrative that illustrates his idiosyncratic decision-making style. It's idiosyncratic in that it's impetuous, often unpredictable, at war with professional government, and often demonstrates limited attention to his problems of political capital. Trump's agenda as well as a discussion of his policy successes and setbacks, at home and abroad, are presented in chapter 6.

How has Trump's presidency reshaped polarization, professional government, popular discontent, and the role of celebrities in national politics? He has reinforced polarization, assaulted professional government, failed to abate popular discontent and may well have ushered in a new era of celebrity politics. Chapter 7 explores each of these impacts with an eye toward Trump's own future. Will he emerge triumphant in a second term, leave office in disrepute or follow a middling course for the remainder of his presidency? The consequences for each of these three possible outcomes for the country's political system receive concluding analysis.

2

OUR TROUBLED PARTIES

Effective political parties are essential for a sound democracy, but American parties have suffered important decline since the 1960s. Party deterioration is a major contributor to the polarization, professionalism, and popular discontent chronicled in chapter 1. It played a role in Donald Trump's nomination and eventual win. In this chapter we reveal the lengthy trend of party unpopularity in public opinion and the growing ideological polarization of the small group of citizens who are party activists.

Parties now act as fundraisers for their candidates, but that important campaign finance role contributes to their unpopularity. "Negative partisanship" by party identifiers motivated by distaste of rival partisans is now a mighty contributor to polarization, but polarization driven by a dislike for the other party can be quite distinct from polarization driven by sharp ideological differences. Polarization driven by one's feelings about or perceptions of the other party can drive voter allegiance to their own party and its candidates even when those candidates are unorthodox or controversial. Taken together, negative partisanship, affective polarization, and a striking "perception gap" are significant elements of contemporary politics and help to explain the inability of the Republican Party apparatus to prevent Trump's rise and eventual win.

PARTIES IN A HISTORICAL CONTEXT

Much of American political history is marked by relatively stable periods of national political dominance by one of the two major political parties. This is what happened in the 1890s when Americans overwhelmingly endorsed the Republican Party. In the election of 1894, for example, Republicans won an additional 130 seats in the House and captured a 254 to 93 seat majority. The election of Republican William McKinley as president in 1896 completed the Republican coup. It marked a thirty-year period of Republican dominance that would not end until the economic collapse of 1929 and the midterm election of 1930 when Democrats came within a seat of reclaiming the House and the Senate. Over the next three elections, Democrats would gain an impressive total of 37 Senate seats and 170 House seats. The overwhelming election of Franklin Roosevelt in 1932 brought about the Democratic dominance that lasted from the early 1930s until the mid-1960s.

Few would have guessed that the election of 1964 would mark the end of the Democratic Party's dominance of American politics. Everything appeared to be breaking the Democrats' way. A clear majority of Americans identified as Democrats, two-thirds of working-class voters identified as Democrats, and at that moment three-quarters of African Americans and just more than seven in ten southern whites expressed allegiance to the Party. Democrat Lyndon Johnson scored a decisive victory over Republican Barry Goldwater, carrying forty-four of the fifty states, plus the District of Columbia, while receiving 61 percent of the national popular vote. Along with the White House, Democrats maintained and expanded their hold on Congress, winning 295 seats in the House to the Republicans' 140. In the Senate, the numbers were sixty-eight Democrats to thirty-two Republicans—Congress had not been so lopsidedly Democratic since the late 1930s.

Beneath the surface of those wins, however, significant changes were taking place that would come to define much of politics and political parties today. Between the 1930s and the 1960s, the Democrats enjoyed their greatest electoral success in southern states and were weakest in the Midwest and New England. The election of 1964 witnessed major changes to those patterns. Johnson lost Louisiana, Mississippi, Alabama, Georgia, and South Carolina. Throughout the south, Johnson's vote margins were below those of Franklin Roosevelt's by double digits. In New England, however, Johnson and the Democrats were surging. In Rhode Island, Massachusetts, Maine, and Vermont the party added roughly twenty-five percentage points to its vote share as compared to FDR's support in the 1936 election. In many ways, the national electoral map was turned upside down as the once solid Democratic south was moving to the GOP and New England, once a bastion of moderate Republicanism, was moving to the Democrats. This shift would have profound effects on the agendas, candidates, and supporters of both parties.

The end of the Democratic Party's lock on the south also marked the end of the Democrats' dominance of national politics. Between 1968 and 2016, Democrats would win the White House in only five of thirteen elections and no Democratic presidential candidate received a majority of the popular vote until Barack Obama in 2008 and 2012. Even Hillary Clinton failed to secure a majority in 2016 despite having won the popular vote against Donald Trump. During this period the Democrats' overwhelming margins and dominance in the House and Senate declined as well. America entered an extremely competitive era in which neither party could lay claim to the sustained allegiance of the American electorate or maintain a hold on power. As a result, partisan control of Congress tended to be temporary and divided government became the norm. Both of these are rare in American history.

Consider partisan control of the White House and the House of Representatives—there was unified party control during fourteen of eighteen Congresses between 1894 and 1928 and during fourteen of nineteen Congresses from 1930 through 1966. The story is quite different now. Unified party control of the House and White House has only existed for eight of the twenty-six Congresses between 1968 and 2018. Divided government has become the rule and not the exception in American politics.

Of the eight Congresses with unified party control, four were controlled by Democrats and four by Republicans.

Consider also the seesaw nature of national elections over the past fifteen years. In 2004, Republican George W. Bush was reelected president and voters elected a Republican controlled House and Senate. In 2006, voters tossed out the GOP and elected a Democratic House and Senate. The Democratic Congress was joined by Barack Obama's win in the 2008 presidential election, but in 2010 voters turned on the Democrats and elected a Republican House majority. Obama was reelected in 2012, but two years later voters handed Senate control to the Republicans. Donald Trump was elected president along with a Republican House and Senate in 2016, but in 2018 voters returned control of the House of Representatives to the Democrats.

We live in an extremely competitive era in which neither party can lay claim to a sustained hold on power or the sustained allegiance of a majority of the voters. According to a May 2019 Gallup poll, 31 percent of American adults identify as Democrats, 30 percent identify as Republicans, and fully 38 percent consider themselves to be independent of the two parties. If independent voters are grouped with the party they most closely identify with, then 44 percent of adults are Republicans and 45 percent are Democrats.[1]

COMPETITION AND POLARIZATION

The increased level of competition has a significant impact on the Democratic and Republican parties and how they work to motivate voters. As American politics became more competitive, the parties became ever more partisan and polarized. Studies confirm that there is a direct and positive connection between party competition and party ideology.[2] Put simply, as a state becomes more competitive between Republicans and Democrats, the respective parties become ever more conservative and liberal as evidenced by issue positions in their respective state party platforms. As competition increases the parties also come to rely more heavily on their base of committed and activist voters—liberal activists for Democrats and conservative activists for Republicans.

According to author and journalist Steven Hill, "one of the defining characteristics of a winner-take-all system is that it promotes adversarial politics so that on a whole host of issues it is painfully obvious that the overriding agenda for both major parties is . . . to stake out positions vis-a-vis the other side."[3] In other words, parties come to identify themselves by adopting positions clearly distinct from those held by the other party. In the 1960s, Republicans exploited several emerging schisms in the ranks of the Democratic coalition in order to become competitive—schisms revolving around national security, welfare spending, and policies regarding race relations. The party defined itself by being what the Democratic Party was not. Over time, both parties increasingly defined themselves by being the antithesis of the other party.

The issue of abortion, as presented in each party's national party platform, offers a telling example of how a party offers a clear contrast with the other party and how partisan activists drive those distinctions. In 1972, abortion rights activists pushed to have a plank added to the Democratic Party platform defending the legality of abortion. Though that initial effort failed, they were able to insert the first supportive abortion language into the platform in 1976 with a mild statement that recognized both the religious and ethical concerns many Americans have with legal abortion while simultaneously expressing support for the court precedent making abortion legal. In 1980, the abortion plank was expanded to make clear that the Democratic Party supported the 1973 *Roe v Wade* ruling in which the Supreme Court determined that women had a right to an abortion. By 1988 the party platform was further expanded to call for the right to an abortion regardless of the ability to pay and in 2008 recognition of religious or ethical objections gave way to an unequivocal statement of support for abortion rights and opposition to any effort to curtail that right.

Changes were taking place in the Republican platform as well. The party's 1976 platform barely mentioned abortion other than the inclusion of a statement endorsing a position on abortion that values human life. In 1980, conservative activists successfully lobbied for a clearer statement. The new position endorsed a Constitutional amendment protecting a right to life for the unborn as well as Congressional action to restrict the use of taxpayer funds to pay for abortions. The new statement also recognized differences of opinion among Americans and Republicans on the issue. By 2008, there could be no doubt regarding the Republican Party's position on abortion as the platform was expanded to include support for judges who respect the sanctity of human life and expressed clear opposition to the use of public funds to promote or perform abortions.

Over the course of three decades, party activists worked to define a Democratic and a Republican Party position regarding abortion that suited their preferences and that were diametrically opposed to each other. It's hard to not see the action and reaction nature of the evolving party platform statements. As electoral competition between the two parties escalated, they responded by drawing ever more distinctions with the other party. These sharp distinctions motivated members of each party's base to donate, turn out, and vote. In more recent years, party activists have worked as well to create clear divisions between the Republican and Democratic parties on issues such as same sex marriage, the regulation of greenhouse gasses, gun ownership, religious freedom, and progressive taxation. The result of all of these "distinctions" is two very polarized political parties.

As the agendas of the political parties became ever more divergent after the 1960s, Americans began to "sort" more neatly into one party or the other, a phenomenon known as *party sorting*. As the Democratic Party became more liberal and the Republican Party more conservative, liberal Republicans left their party and became Democrats or independents and conservative Democrats became Republicans or independents. Evidence of party polarization has been well documented, especially among the most active and informed voters and within elective bodies such as the US Congress.[4] Data from the General Social Survey,[5] which has been measuring US public opinion since 1972, makes clear the full effect of party sorting. Consider the issue of abortion. In 1978 roughly one-third of Democrats and one-third of Republicans agreed that a woman should have a legal right to an abortion for any reason. In 2018 things looked very different as two-thirds of Democrats agreed with the legality of abortion for any reason as compared to just more than one-quarter of Republicans. Over the course of four decades, pro-life Democrats left the Democratic Party and pro-choice Republicans left their party.

As one might expect, the self-described ideology of Republicans and Democrats changed as well. In 1978 27 percent of Democrats identified as conservative, 41 percent as moderate, and fewer than a third identified as liberal. Among Republicans, one in five identified as liberal and 35 percent identified as moderate. In 2018, fewer than one in six Democrats identified as conservative and fewer than one-third as moderate. Over 55 percent of Democrats identified as liberal. Among Republicans in 2018, roughly 7 percent identified as liberal, fewer than one-quarter as moderate, and over two-thirds identified as conservative. How do we know that these changes reflect party sorting and not changes in the ideological beliefs of all Americans? Because the ideological beliefs of all Americans are roughly the same today as in 1978. In 1978 just shy of 30 percent of Americans identified as being liberal and roughly one-third identified as conservative. The remaining 40 percent described themselves as moderate. Fast forward to 2018 and just shy of 30 percent of Americans identified as being liberal and roughly one-third identified as conservative. The remaining 40 percent described themselves as moderate. During that same four decades, the share of Americans identifying as independent increased and the share of independents identifying as moderate increased significantly.

Over the past several decades, liberal and conservative activists have worked to redefine the political parties in their ideological images. On a host of issues ranging from health care, taxation, welfare spending, abortion, and same sex marriage, the parties are increasingly defined by their stark contrasts with one another. As the differences between the two parties became ever clearer, voters responded by more neatly sorting into the two camps. The overall electorate is no more divided by ideology today than it was thirty years ago, but the two political parties are much more divided, and that division defines contemporary politics and discourse. Ideology and partisanship need not be synonymous and for much of the twentieth century prior to the late 1960s they were not. But today, it is understandable why many equate partisan Democrat with ideological liberal and partisan Republican with ideological conservative. And given that American politics is dominated by those two parties, the ideological sorting that has taken place translates into deeply divided political battles and creates the appearance of an increasingly ideological electorate.

NEGATIVE PARTISANSHIP, AFFECTIVE POLARIZATION, AND THE PERCEPTION GAP

The stark ideological differences emphasized by Democratic and Republican elites coupled with the growing ideological homogeneity of each party has given rise to forms of polarization and partisanship derived not necessarily from ideology but rather by perceptions of and attitudes toward the other party. These perceptions and attitudes help to explain how Donald Trump was able to secure the support of Republicans even as he was rather new to the party and held views that ran counter to established party doctrine. Discussions of contemporary American politics tend to center around the issue of polarization and the notion that Americans are deeply divided over a host of issues. This yawning division is driving our elected officials to eschew cooperation and compromise. There is a robust debate among political scientists regarding the true nature of polarization in American. Regardless of that debate, it is clear the ideological divide between self-identified Democrats and self-identified Republicans among both elected officials and the electorate has grown.

Given that most Democrats are also liberals and most Republicans are also conservatives, they are less likely to encounter partisan peers with different political ideas. Though polarization and party sorting may result in some partisans liking their own party more and the other party less, it is also possible some partisans may be displeased with the direction their party has embraced but may not be willing to alter their partisan allegiance. Under such circumstances, these partisans may adopt a "lesser of two evils" approach to partisanship in which they convince themselves that the other party remains far worse than their own. As such, continued allegiance to their own party seems to them justified.[6]

Under this understanding of partisan loyalty, it's quite possible for a voter to become more loyal to their party even as their confidence or satisfaction with their party falls. All that matters is that their animosity toward the opposing party grows at a rate that exceeds their frustrations with their own party. There is evidence to suggest that this has been happening. Since the 1970s the American National Election Studies has measured partisans' feelings toward their own party on a scale ranging from 0 (very cold) to 100 (very warm). The higher the reported score, the more a partisan likes their party. The data show that Republicans and Democrats have cooled to their own parties over the course of the last forty years. Until recently, there was little variation among partisans regarding their feelings toward their own party, but recent years have witnessed greater variation with a rise in the share of partisans reporting warm feelings as well as those reporting cooler feelings. This variation suggests that some partisans are pleased with the ideological polarization that defines their party and are reporting warmer feelings while others are unhappy with it and reporting cooler feelings.

As a result of this lack of exposure, people are likely to see members of the other party as different and their beliefs as less normal. This party sorting and separation may lead partisans to view members of the other party as more extreme than they really are. A 2019 study found this *perception gap* can be significant. Self-identified Democrats and Republicans believe that 55 percent of their opponents hold extreme views, but in reality only about 30 percent of partisans hold such views.[7] The perception gap is greatest among the most committed partisans. The wider a person's perception gap, the more likely they are to attribute negative personal qualities to members of the other party. The same study found that 84 percent of Republicans described Democrats as "hateful" and 87 percent described them as "brainwashed." Fully 71 percent of Republicans described Democrats as "racist." Perceptions were not any better among Democrats. Approximately nine out of ten Democrats described Republicans as hateful (87 percent), brainwashed (88 percent), and racist (89 percent).[8]

Party sorting has made it much easier for partisans to make generalized inferences about members of the other party, even if those inferences are woefully incorrect or distorted. The perception gap is so powerful that it can drive polarization between the parties based not on ideology but rather a partisan's affect toward the other party. Affective polarization refers to the tendency of self-identified partisans to view opposing partisans negatively.[9] One fascinating aspect of affective polarization is that it may promote partisan loyalty even when partisans do not particularly like their own party. A study by political scientist Eric Groenendyke found very little evidence to support claims of mass polarization along ideological lines. Rather, he found widespread policy agreement among Americans on all but a few issues. In an equally surprising finding, he determined there is no evidence of Americans becoming more attached to their parties. Instead, he finds few people love, or even like, their own party or think it represents their interests well.

So what drives their party loyalty? Their hatred of the other party. This hate is enough to keep Americans loyal to their respective parties. In fact, the more frustrated people become with their own party, the more they denounce and demonize the *other* party. Why? Demonizing the other party makes voters feel better about sticking with their own party even if their party doesn't do a good job representing their views. It is in this way that affective polarization drives what is known as negative partisanship, or party loyalty driven by anger toward and dislike of an opposing party.[10]

Consumption of news, especially from biased sources, as well as exposure to social media such as Twitter and Facebook are fueling a perception gap that furthers affective polarization and negative partisanship. Among

Republicans, those who followed Sean Hannity or Rush Limbaugh or consumed news from the Drudge Report had the largest perception gaps toward Democrats. For Democrats, relying on *Slate*, Daily Kos, Buzzfeed, or the *Huffington Post* led to significant perception gaps. How does social media fuel the perception gap? According to analysis by Pew, only 10 percent of Twitter users are responsible for 80 percent of the posts to the social media platform. Those who post about politics to social media have a significantly larger perception gap than those who do not post.[11] As a result, those distorted perceptions of partisans are more likely to be posted to social media and read by users of a specific platform. It should not be surprising then to learn that roughly 64 percent of Democrats and 55 percent of Republicans say they have "just a few" or "no" close friends who are from the other political party.[12]

At first glance, one may assume that affective polarization and negative partisanship fueled by a perception gap benefits the Democratic and Republican parties by producing party loyalty. The opposite is likely true. This type of polarization and partisanship can be especially limiting on the two parties and their ability to govern. Negative partisanship drives people to vote *against* the other party instead of *for* their own party. Given this electoral reality, parties and candidates focus less on unifying voters around a cohesive and forward-looking agenda and instead seek to maximize "fear and loathing" toward the opposing party in order to win elections.

As a result, the winning party receives no real mandate to govern. Rather, once the other party loses, voters tend to focus on the reasons why they dislike their own party. Now in an era when divided government is the norm, cooperation between the parties may be necessary to address the problems of the day. But compromise and cooperation prove to be elusive in an era when voters of one party view the other party not as a partner in governance but as a dishonest, nasty enemy to be defeated.

This can limit severely a party's ability to govern even under a period of unified government. Republicans enjoyed unified government for the first two years of Donald Trump's presidency, yet they struggled to generate meaningful legislative accomplishments. During the 2016 campaign Trump repeatedly promised to repeal and replace the Affordable Care Act, but neither Trump nor Congressional Republicans were ever able to coalesce around replacement legislation that could pass in the Republican controlled House as well as the Republican controlled Senate. The failure to develop a suitable replacement plan ultimately sunk the repeal effort. Indeed, polls showed that despite the Republican victories in 2016 and a pledge by the party for GOP candidates to repeal and replace the Affordable Care Act, dating back to 2010, a majority of Americans opposed repealing the law. Trump faced similar dead ends in his effort to secure funding to build a wall along the American border with Mexico as well as funding for infrastructure improvements. In the end, the only significant legislative victory produced by two years of unified government was the 2017 Tax Cuts and Jobs Act which reduced tax rates and introduced other reforms intended to simplify the tax code. Though heralded by Trump as a major achievement, polls show that barely one-third of Americans approve of the legislation.[13]

NEGATIVE PARTISANSHIP, POPULIST ANGER, AND THE 2016 ELECTION

In many ways, the 2016 Democratic and Republican primaries demonstrated the challenges that negative partisanship created for both parties. Political scientist Eric Groenendyk sums up the implications of all of this quite well: "Republicans and Democrats have divided against one another, but not necessarily into more cohesive teams. . . . If partisans' identities are increasingly anchored to hatred of the out party rather than affection for their own party, electoral dynamics are likely much more fluid than many accounts suggest. Thus, insurgent candidates with questionable ideological credentials may be more appealing than one might expect in the age of ideologically sorted parties."[14]

Two months before Donald Trump descended the escalator in Trump Tower to announce his outsider campaign for the Republican nomination for president, another outsider had announced his run for the Democratic nomination. On April 30, 2015, Vermont Senator Bernie Sanders proclaimed his candidacy during a press conference outside the US Capitol. What made Sanders's announcement particularly newsworthy was the simple fact that he was not a registered Democrat. Sanders has represented the state of Vermont since 1990, first in the House and then in the Senate, as an independent candidate who identifies as a Democratic Socialist. The 2016 nominating primary was the very first Democratic primary, for any office, in which Sanders participated. During his forty years in office, he has frequently run against and defeated Democratic nominees. Sanders also was a frequent critic of the Democratic Party, describing it at times as "ideologically bankrupt" and once declaring "I am not a Democrat, period." Though Sanders caucuses with the Democrats in the US Senate, when asked in the past about joining the party Sanders rhetorically asked, "Why should we work within the Democratic Party if we don't agree with anything the Democratic Party says?"[15]

Much as Bernie Sanders was an outsider running for the nomination of a party to which he did not belong, Donald Trump was an outsider running for the nomination of a Republican Party to which his attachment seemed more opportunistic than ideological. Though Trump had flirted with Republican presidential politics in the 1990s, New York City voter records show that Trump was registered as a Democrat from 2001 until 2009. During the primary, Trump explained his Democratic past to CNN saying "it just seems that the economy does better under the Democrats than the Republicans."[16] In addition to the Democratic Party, Trump was once registered with the Independence Party—the party that grew from Ross Perot's independent presidential runs in the 1990s. Trump even made threats that he would run as an independent candidate in 2016 if he was denied the Republican nomination. And as a candidate, Trump railed against what he viewed as the Republican Party's failed trade strategies and embraced a commitment to entitlement programs like Social Security as well as increased infrastructure spending that was more closely aligned with Democrats.

Sanders and Trump tapped into the angry politics detailed in chapter 1 and channeled voter frustration with a distant and professionalized politics into two very effective insurgent campaigns. In the end, only Trump was successful. This isn't entirely surprising. Democrats, as the pro-statist party, suffer more from the ongoing crisis of confidence in government than do Republicans. However, since the 1960s, every crisis, except 9/11, has served to erode public confidence—the savings and loan crisis of the late 1980s, the government shutdowns of the mid-1990s, the second Iraq War, the subprime mortgage crisis and Troubled Asset Relief Program of 2008, and the battles over the debt ceiling since 2011. It's possible that at some point a crisis will occur that will demand a reenergized governmental system. Thus far, however, crises have served only to reinforce the dominant narrative of ineffective governance.

Since the New Deal, the Democrats have been the party of government. Democratic voters are more likely to believe that government can make things better. Following eight years of Barack Obama, most Democrats believed that government was on the right track. To many Democrats, Sanders's insurgency was a threat to the past eight years of accomplishments and they did not believe that revolution, called for by Sanders, was necessary. Sanders failed as well because he had a clear agenda that Clinton could run against. Unlike other political philosophies, populism is less about offering a pro-active agenda of policies and is instead focused on mobilizing the public in reaction against the status quo and politics as usual. Democrats in 2016 were mostly happy with the status quo established by Barack Obama and Clinton promised to hold true to Obama's legacy and to build upon it. Exit polls show that on Election Day Clinton's voters approved of President Obama's job performance and wanted the next president to continue Obama's policies. Revolution was not what most Democrats wanted.

The Tea Party movement grew and evolved. It elected members to Congress and played a significant role in propelling Trump during the early days of his campaign when many did not take him seriously. The Occupy Wall Street movement, on the other hand, never evolved beyond a nebulous political movement devoid of a unifying agenda or organizational center. This suggests that Democrats and Democratic leaning voters were more satisfied with the direction of the country. Surveys confirm Democrats were more satisfied than Republicans with the direction of the country and far more likely to believe that the country was on the right track during the Obama presidency. In the spring of 2016, barely a third of Americans believed that the country was on the right track, but the difference between Republicans and Democrats was stark. Fully 90 percent of Republicans believed that the country was moving in the wrong direction as compared to less than half of Democrats. The Republican Party offered more fertile ground for a populist movement.

Sanders and his supporters promised an economic agenda billed as a dramatic departure from what the Democratic Party had offered since the 1980s. Sanders pledged to eliminate private health insurance and replace it with "Medicare-for-all" single-payer health care, doubling the federal minimum wage from $7.25 to $15 an hour, providing free tuition at public colleges and universities, large-scale public investments to build a clean-energy economy and rebuild the crumbling US infrastructure, an end to free trade agreements like the North American Free Trade Agreement (NAFTA), and strong Wall Street regulations. This created an opportunity for Clinton to present herself to Democratic voters as a safe or moderate choice who could achieve policy objectives without tearing at the very foundations of the Democratic Party. Clinton positioned herself as a steady and pragmatic leader who promised to build on the gains made under Obama. Where Sanders promised revolution, Clinton promised pragmatic progress. Clinton warned that Medicare for all would never happen and that a debate over it would jeopardize the Affordable Care Act. To Sanders's promise of free tuition Clinton countered with a plan targeting families earning less than $125,000 per year. When

Sanders attacked Planned Parenthood, NARAL Pro-Choice America, and the Human Rights Campaign as "the establishment" after they endorsed Clinton, a traditional populist strategy, it backfired as most Democrats viewed such entities as crucial partners.

That does not mean that Sanders failed to mount a serious challenge. In the summer of 2015, Clinton was viewed as the presumptive nominee of the Democratic Party. Bernie Sanders was polling at 10 percent or below. Much had changed by the time of the Iowa Caucuses where Sanders finished just within two-tenths of 1 percent behind Clinton. One week later Sanders crushed Clinton by a twenty-two-point margin in the New Hampshire Primary. Clinton was able to regain momentum and right the ship when the primary contests moved south, but in the end, Sanders carried twenty-three contests and received 43 percent of the total primary vote to Clinton's thirty-four wins and 55 percent of the primary vote. Sanders had an impact. In the end, there simply wasn't enough populist rage on the left to beat back Hillary Clinton and the party establishment.

That was not the case for Trump and the Republican Party. After eight years of Obama, most Republicans were angry. They viewed establishment Republicans like Speaker of the House Paul Ryan and Senate Majority Leader Mitch McConnell as sellouts unwilling, or incapable, of taking on Obama or the Democrats. Republican voters were receptive to Trump's repeated assaults on the Republican establishment, the Democratic establishment, and any other establishment that raised his ire. As discussed in chapter 4, Trump very effectively used this to his advantage when establishment Republicans began to explore ways to deny him the nomination at the party convention. Trump's agenda, such as it was, maximized populist energy by focusing on issues that mattered to working- and middle-class Republicans like protecting Social Security, securing the borders, and ending the outsourcing of jobs. How he would accomplish these things was rarely discussed.

In the general election matchup with Clinton, Trump continued to rail against the establishment. Clinton pursued the strategy that had helped her to defeat Sanders—pragmatism as opposed to revolution. Both candidates relied heavily on negative partisanship and the perception gap to motivate voters. Clinton warned voters that Trump was too dangerous and unstable to possess the nuclear codes and that his "thin skin" could lead America into war.[17] In June 2016, Clinton took to Twitter, Trump's favorite communication device to warn "Imagine if he had not just his Twitter account at his disposal when he's angry, but America's entire arsenal." Trump portrayed Clinton as a criminal who would be subject to nonstop investigations and her presidency would end in a Constitutional crisis. He said her protection of the Affordable Care Act would destroy American health care forever. In perhaps his harshest attack, he warned that Clinton's commitment to stopping ISIS in Syria would lead to World War III with Russia. In effect, both candidates had warned that the other might bring about the end of the world.

Party elites and candidates often seek to motivate partisans by painting every election as a choice between political life and death. But the rhetoric in 2016 had escalated considerably since the closing days of the 2000 election when Al Gore suggested that "strict constructionists" like George W. Bush are little different from those who once deemed a black man to be but three-fifths of a person. Or the waning days of the 2008 campaign when Sarah Palin accused Barack Obama of "palling around with terrorists" because of his association with former Weather Underground founder, and eventual college professor and political activist, Bill Ayers. The ante has been upped in the contest to motivate voters in such a closely matched era. The goal for Democrats and Republicans is often the same—scare the heck out of the party base in an effort to motivate them. As a result, the left reduces the right to a caricature of bigoted, racist, violent, homophobic fascists and the right reduces the left to a caricature of immoral, anti-American, authoritarian socialists. The hope is that the scare tactics will motivate the base and win over enough wavering voters in the middle to prevail come Election Day.

In 2016 very few voters were pleased with the presidential candidates offered by the two major political parties. Trump and Clinton were the least popular presidential candidates ever polled. On Election Day, 55 percent of voters had an unfavorable opinion of Clinton and 60 percent an unfavorable opinion of Trump. Many observers assumed that Trump's higher negatives would be his undoing. Although both candidates received the vote of 95 percent of voters with a favorable opinion of them, Trump received support from 81 percent of voters with an unfavorable view of Clinton. Clinton received support from only 77 percent of voters with an unfavorable opinion of Trump. Nearly one in five voters viewed both Trump and Clinton unfavorably, but Trump won those voters by a seventeen-point margin. In other words, Trump and Clinton fared equally well among the voters who liked them, but Trump did noticeably better among voters who disliked them.

Think of it this way. Many folks who voted for Trump did not care what policies he proposed or focus on his character flaws. They cared that he wasn't a Democrat. And many voted against him not because of who he was or love of Clinton but because he was a Republican. That means that should he run for reelection, many voters will be motivated to vote against the Democrat with little care for what Trump has done or not done while in office. As a result, it may not even matter to many Republican or Republican leaning voters if Trump is impeached by the House (assuming he's not convicted by the Senate). According to exit polls, full one-quarter of all voters in 2016 said that they voted for their candidate because they disliked the opponent. Trump carried those voters 50 percent to 39 percent over Clinton. Nearly two-thirds of voters said Trump was neither honest and trustworthy nor qualified to be president and yet one in five of those voters voted for Trump.

It's clear that a substantial number of voters on Election Day were driven by populist anger or negative partisanship—or both. This suggests that Trump's frequent tirades against Republicans as well as Democrats may be a very effective way to keep his base happy and motivated going into 2020. But the 2018 midterm elections show that anger and negative partisanship can cut both ways. With Trump in the White House and the Senate in Republican hands, Trump has achieved a substantial restructuring of the federal judiciary. Successful confirmation battles putting Neil Gorsuch and Brett Kavanaugh on the Supreme Court motivated Democratic voters. In the 2018 midterms, Democrats reclaimed control of the House of Representatives by flipping forty-three Republican-held seats and limiting Democratic losses to two seats. Of the forty-three seats flipped, more than two dozen were in districts that Trump had won in 2016.

That's clear evidence of motivation against Republicans. It's estimated that more than four million Obama voters from 2012 stayed home in 2016. They may have been convinced that Trump could not win or they may have been unhappy with Clinton. Though we do not know why they stayed home, we do know that they were disproportionately young and African American—both key Democratic constituencies.[18] It is likely that these voters will be more motivated in 2020, either by support for their party's nominee or by their opposition to Trump and Republicans.

The 2018 midterms, however, were not all bad news for Trump. Though Democrats did flip well over three dozen seats, they failed to achieve the same level of gains realized by Republicans in 1994 or 2010. During the past seventy years, except for Bill Clinton in 1998, the party in the White House has always lost seats in the House of Representatives during the first midterm of an incumbent president. The Democrats' seat gains were expected, but not exceptional. Republicans, however, gained seats in the Senate. For most of the year preceding the 2018 midterms there had been a notable "enthusiasm gap" with Democratic voters far more interested in voting in the election. However much the controversial Kavanaugh confirmation hearings may have motivated Democrats, it's clear that it caused Republican voters to reengage and close the enthusiasm gap.[19] Once again, negative partisanship cuts both ways.

Turnout for the 2018 midterms hit a fifty-year high, but turnout was up for both parties not just the party out of power. Negative partisanship virtually ensures Democrats and Republicans will be motivated to vote come 2020. A May 2019 Gallup poll found 31 percent of American adults identify as Democrats and 30 percent identify as Republicans, and if independent voters are grouped with the party they most closely identify with then, 44 percent of adults are Republicans and 45 percent

CHAPTER 2

are Democrats. Polarization and intense two-party competition suggest a close race for president in 2020.

Indications are that Trump intends to repeat in 2020 much of the strategy used to secure victory in 2016. With historically high negatives, Trump and his campaign team understood that he would not win a popularity contest. Instead, the focus was on winning a contest among the unpopular. Polarization and negative partisanship would deliver Trump a significant share of votes, but likely not enough to secure victory. Trump needed to win over some voters who may have been deeply uncomfortable with him. Enter the politics of "whataboutism." Any time Trump was accused of doing something inappropriate or even criminal, Trump would deflect and point the finger at the opposition. When the Trump Foundation was accused of being a Trump slush fund Trump responded by attacking the Clinton Global Initiative with a similar charge. When Trump was accused of inappropriate behavior and outright sexual assault, he responded by pointing to the women who had accused Bill Clinton of the same. During his presidency when he has been accused of racism, he quickly counters by referring to his accusers as racists.

When the House of Representatives opened an impeachment inquiry in response to President Trump's July 2019 phone call with Ukrainian President Zelensky in which Trump asked Zelensky to work with the US Attorney General as well as Trump's personal attorney to investigate unsubstantiated allegations of wrongdoing by a potential political rival, Trump and his defenders responded by accusing Hillary Clinton and former President Obama of being the ones who colluded with foreign governments. Trump and his supporters deflected the charges by claiming that the real story was the supposed wrongdoing by his potential rival. It didn't matter that these allegations and deflections were baseless, what mattered was that they muddied the water and confused the public.

Trump understands that many voters are deeply uncomfortable with his character and behavior and are therefore reluctant to vote for him. By relying on the politics of whataboutism, Trump offers these voters an out. If these hesitant voters are convinced that both sides are flawed and imperfect, then perhaps they can better justify a vote for Trump. Trump once again understands that he will not win a popularity contest in 2020, so he wants to repeat the contest between unpopular choices that propelled him to victory in 2016.

IS THE PARTY OVER?

The Republican Party establishment spent the last half of 2015 and the first quarter of 2016 trying to derail Trump's quest for the party's nomination for president. Not only did those efforts fail, they appear to have galvanized Trump's support among the rank and file. Trump has taken on and cast aside long-standing Republican issues such as free trade and entitlement reform. Former critics, and 2016 opponents, such as Senators Ted Cruz (R-TX), Marco Rubio (R-FL), and Lindsey Graham (R-SC) now routinely defend and even praise Trump. The president has installed his team at the Republican National Committee, and he enjoys the support of over 90 percent of Republicans. Impeachment is likely to be the ultimate test of Trump's control over his party.

On the Democratic side, roughly twenty thousand emails illegally obtained by Wikileaks and released to the press make clear that the Democratic National Committee (DNC) wanted to see Sanders fail and that some officials discussed ways to undermine his campaign. Although Sanders did lose, the Wikileaks revelations led to the resignation of the DNC chair— Clinton ally Debbie Wasserman Schultz. Under pressure from Sanders and his supporters, the DNC changed the party's nominating process by eliminating first ballot voting by so-called superdelegates, a group of roughly seven hundred party (establishment) leaders, elected officials, and activists who were free to back any candidate they chose for the nomination. In a close race, these establishment delegates could determine the nomination outcome. Sanders again sought the party nomination for 2020.

What does all of this mean for the future of the two major parties? The modern nominating process, created in 1972, allows candidates to bypass the party establishment and appeal directly to voters who then make a choice via primary or caucus. There's precious little that a party can do to prevent a candidate from seeking a party nomination and even less that can be done once a candidate secures a nomination. This is especially true of presidential nominations and once a candidate secures a party nomination for president, they tend to have the power to remake party procedures and agendas. Negative partisanship raised the specter of voters motivated not by love or respect for their own party but rather serious dislike for the other party. That's hardly a recipe for party strength.

In his farewell address to Congress, President George Washington offered harsh words for political parties and their "baneful effects." Washington warned that the "alternate domination of one faction over another, sharpened by the spirit of revenge . . . serves always to distract the public councils and enfeeble the public administration. It agitates the community with ill-founded jealousies and false alarms, kindles the animosity of one part against another."[20] No doubt many today share Washington's dim view of parties. Negative partisanship and affective polarization raise questions of whether a party victory represented an endorsement of that party's agenda or simply a rejection of the other party's agenda. That, coupled with intense and close party competition, discourages compromise and often yields policy stalemate even when one party enjoys unified control of government.

It's important to remember, though, that the parties still matter. In fact, it's nearly impossible to imagine any representative democracy functioning without them. Parties exist as the primary organizing force in government. Party is what binds one member of Congress to another and party is what builds bridges (or walls) between the legislative and executive branch. The parties perform important administrative roles in elections, including the organization of primaries, the creation of a party platform, and voter outreach. Parties create the very competition that drives elections. Parties create a link between elected officials and the public. The nature of that link and the role that parties play has changed, but they remain a critical component of American politics.

3

TRUMP THE
CELEBRITY

The *Merriam-Webster Online Dictionary* defines celebrity as "the state of being celebrated; fame" and "a famous or celebrated person." Donald Trump has spent his adult lifetime pursuing both definitions of the word, seeking fame as a celebrated person. He has succeeded to an extent few would have predicted when he got his start in New York real estate in the late 1970s.

Writing before Trump gained the White House, media critic Neal Gabler explained contemporary celebrity a bit further, describing it as "human entertainment . . . a person who, by the very process of *living* provided entertainment for us—a definition that embraces . . . businessmen like Donald Trump."[1] For Gabler, the narrative provided by a celebrity's life is the key source of fame.

Donald Trump has spent his entire adult life crafting a narrative that gains and keeps public attention. Why? His personality made it an essential life quest. He also viewed fame as vital to business success. At several key moments, celebrity boosted trump's financial and political fortunes. It proved a good bet for him.

The Trump approach to celebrity has several features. First, his search for the spotlight is constant, occupying much of Trump's time and energy since his career began over forty years ago. Second, Trump alone directs his celebrity efforts. Though he has hired public relations assistants, ultimately Donald Trump has always taken charge of his personal publicity campaign. Third, it involves antics and verbal eruptions beyond the ken of most people. Trump has had few compunctions about how he kept in the public eye, resorting to sex talk on Howard Stern's radio show, fake battles in the ring of the Word Wrestling Federation, and sponsorship of multiple beauty pageants. He has invited coverage by supermarket tabloids of his divorces and affairs, operated several prominent casinos, and used Twitter to issue venomous attacks on those arousing his ire. Fourth, Trump's attention-getting behavior has regularly involved exaggerations and falsehoods, employed for sensational effect.

It's striking that Trump's modus operandi has changed little since he became president. But what gained him attention for decades in America's pop culture does not always translate well in governing circles, as we'll note later in this book. It did help him get elected in the first place, and that resulted from a steadily growing celebrity power in national politics.

THE RISE OF CELEBRITY POWER

America's media environment has always shaped the life of celebrities. Available means of communication determine who gets famous, for what reasons and for how long. The invention of the telegraph in the 1840s allowed better and quicker national dissemination of news, allowing newspapers to spotlight national trends and colorful personalities. An accomplished early practitioner of the art of celebrity was Phineas Taylor Barnum.

Barnum's career had a descendant in Trump's celebrity exploits. The medium of the day was newspapers, and Barnum, with his newspaper experience, used them to great advantage in publicizing his activities and shows. Barnum began as a small business owner and eventually founded a weekly newspaper. From there, he expanded into a variety of attention-getting activities, much like Trump did many decades later. Early in his career he published an autobiography extolling his achievements and in subsequent years continued to write attention-getting books—also like Trump. Barnum pioneered constant and sensational publicity for his enterprises. He ran a traveling variety troupe and owned a museum of remarkable and at times fraudulent curiosities, like the "feejee mermaid," constructed with a monkey head and fish tail. He sponsored blackface minstrel shows, a nationwide tour of the "Swedish nightingale" soprano Jenny Lind, and eventually owned and operated a celebrated "world's greatest" circus. Along the way he dabbled in politics, serving as mayor of Bridgeport, Connecticut, and in the state legislature.

Donald Trump is a showman whose career involved a wide variety of attention-getting activities in the Barnum mold. Trump used two trends in today's media environment to great advantage. First, new technologies, from cable television in the 1970s to the internet in the 1990s and social media after 2000 have empowered audiences, providing a growing market for the media's presentation of celebrities. An explosion of "reality television" involving celebrities in challenging situations followed, creating a great opportunity for Trump. Second, the public demand for celebrities has further empowered the celebrities themselves, making them more autonomous and providing them opportunities to express themselves politically.[2]

Donald Trump made good use of both of these trends, constantly presenting himself and his activities in a growing market for celebrities. He always kept personal control of his celebrity activities. This made his move into politics, accomplished at the apex of his celebrity after fifteen years starring in *The Apprentice* television show, a relatively smooth move.

The power of contemporary celebrities arises from three traits that Trump painstakingly developed. First is the ability to employ and control information. Social media, staged events, speeches, and interviews provide this control. Trump over the years pursued all these avenues to spotlight issues, employ emotional appeals and endorse causes and candidates. Second, celebrities can persuasively, personally identify with their audiences. Aristotle termed this "ethos" defined as the ability of a speaker to persuade an audience through personal identification. Trump speaks in an informal and unvarnished vernacular that is similar to that employed by many in his audience. His talk helps him to seem "authentic" and "one of us." Third, celebrities can muster "symbolic identification" with concepts that the target audience holds dear. The American flag, always near Trump in his public appearances as candidate and president, and his 2016 campaign slogan "Make America Great Again" illustrate his effective display of appealing symbols and slogans.[3]

Trump is an exemplar of the power of contemporary celebrity in American politics. He uses the tools of celebrity—information, identification, and symbols—to great effect. At the center of it all is Trump and his personality. Understanding those personal traits leads us to the origins of the celebrity tempest that is Donald Trump.

BECOMING DONALD TRUMP

Donald Trump entered this world on June 14, 1946, the fourth of five children of Fred and Mary MacLeod Trump.[4] Fred was a successful Queens real estate developer and landlord, a millionaire by the time of Donald's birth. Mary was a Scottish immigrant with an attraction to pageantry. Donald later admitted that his flair for showmanship probably came from his mother. His father instilled in him an imperative for hard work, involving him in property maintenance and rent collection as he was growing up. Trump's career-long workaholism reflects his father's industriousness. That workaholism appeared in Donald's later, relentless pursuit of publicity and celebrity.

Donald Trump has been self-absorbed since his earliest days. His older sister Maryanne, a retired federal judge, recalls that her little brother was headstrong and full of mischief: "We used to call him, when he was a little kid, the great I-am."[5] Young Donald also evidenced aggressive behavior on the athletic field and with his teachers and peers. He argued with his father about the strict rules in their home. In seventh grade he would sneak off to Manhattan with his friend Peter Brant. The two boys each assembled a personal collection of switchblade knives.

Fred Trump discovered the knives and he and Mary decided Donald needed a big dose of discipline. As Donald's eighth grade year began, they shipped him off to New York Military Academy. Donald's initial months at the academy were rough. He received physical punishment from his superior officers and classmates. Gradually, Donald adapted to the system. As his high school years passed, he became a leading student at the academy, doing well academically and excelling as a first baseman on the school's team. Visions of future celebrity enticed him. "I'm going to be famous one day" he told a classmate.

His showmanship surfaced in several ways. He brought beautiful women to campus to show them around the place and invite the envy of classmates. In his senior yearbook, he is labeled a "ladies' man." His aggression also appeared as he rose in the academy's ranks. At times he smacked junior schoolmates and once almost tossed a messy student out a second floor window. Rough behavior was not that uncommon in the academy's student ranks back then. By his senior year, Trump was promoted to captain of A Company and commanded the academy's special drill team for New York City's Columbus Day parade. His parents beamed with pride over his accomplishments at the academy.

Donald then enrolled in Fordham University, a Catholic school in the Bronx, because he did not want to be far from home while in college. On campus, he was pretty much a "straight arrow," dressing well and avoiding drugs or alcohol. After two years at Fordham, he transferred to the University of Pennsylvania's Wharton School of Business. There he focused on a career in real estate and ignored the inflammatory campus issues of the 1960s. His two years in Philadelphia constitute the only time he lived outside of New York City before entering the White House. In the small real estate department, Trump talked big to his student peers, promising grand success. During the summers he worked in his father's real estate business.

Though he later claimed to graduate at the top of his class, his name never appeared on the school's honor roll, nor did his fellow students remember him as academically outstanding.

Donald initially worked for his father's firm, Trump Management, overseeing fourteen thousand apartments throughout the outer boroughs of New York City. By the time he turned twenty-five in 1971, he was president of the privately held company, with his father now serving as chairman. The younger Trump, however, had long had his sights set on Manhattan. He soon moved to a small Manhattan apartment and commuted to Trump Management in Queens. After settling a contentious racial discrimination suit against Trump Management, he was ready to launch his own enterprise in the Manhattan real estate market.

Trump got a membership in the exclusive Le Club, befriended controversial lawyer Roy Cohn, and presented himself as the head of a substantial—but imaginary—real estate firm, The Trump Organization. Trump recalled: "When I moved to Manhattan to do my first deal, I did not have money or employees. When I went into an office, I acted as if I had an organization, The Trump Organization, behind me. . . . Few people knew that The Trump Organization had no employees except myself and operated out of my studio apartment in Manhattan."[6] The key was the appearance of experience and competence, of putting up a good front, orchestrating a good show. That, plus hard work and bad mouthing rivals—an early, well-established Trump trait—was his formula for achievement.

In 1976, Donald "settled down" to marriage with his first wife, Ivana, a Czech-born former model, being careful first to get her signature on a prenuptial agreement. Their wedding reception followed at the 21 Club, long known as a celebrity hangout. The new couple appeared at trendy spots, including the opening of Studio 54, the center of the new disco dance craze. Trump added his wife to his executive staff, where she worked decorating and managing properties for him. Their three children—Donald Jr., Ivanka, and Eric—would mainly encounter their father through visits to his office.

From 1975 to 1987, Donald Trump climbed his way to prominence in Manhattan real estate. He did not start from scratch, as he often later claimed. Father Fred loaned him $350,000 to get started. Donald's workaholic and abstemious ways contributed to his rise, but so did his constant pursuit of publicity. The result was renown for him and his successes, which gradually accumulated over the years.

An early Manhattan effort was his proposal to build a convention center on 34th Street. But he was young with no buildings erected yet, ranking about zero on the celebrity scale. The press conference he held at the site attracted not a single reporter. All that changed after his successful effort to transform the seedy Commodore Hotel near Grand Central Station into the glittering Grand Hyatt, a project he undertook with the Hyatt hotel chain.

The area around Grand Central was bedraggled. Then bankrupt Penn Central railroad owned the decrepit hotel. Trump convinced public officials that renovation was important to the neighborhood and city and garnered a forty-year tax abatement. With such government support, he was able to arrange bank financing, bringing the major project in under budget and ahead of schedule. Father Fred proved essential to the project, cosigning key construction contracts, but Donald has never called attention to his father's role. The young developer's reputation as a savior of the neighborhood insured him the plentiful publicity he desired for subsequent projects.

Trump soon "went big" planning a huge luxury residential tower at 57th Street and Fifth Avenue with a remarkable glass exterior and expensive decorations, fittings and finishes throughout. The gaudiness of the project prompted his father's disapproval. When it opened in 1983, though, it instantly became a landmark. Donald took the opportunity to name it Trump Tower, the first of many buildings that would showcase his last name.

Another project that bestowed much attention on Trump was his renovation of the Wollman ice skating rink in Central Park in 1986. The city had already spent $20 million on the project yet it was far from completion.

Boasting that he could finish it and save money in the process, he undertook renovations that were completed in four months and $750,000 under budget. Trump initiated multiple press conferences throughout the project, helping to burnish his growing reputation.

The successes of the Commodore renovation, Trump Tower, and the Wollman rink gave Donald Trump a big taste of fame—and he liked it. It was time to spread his name beyond the confines of New York City. A personal business biography in print would accomplish that.

THE ART OF THE DEAL

Publisher Si Newhouse noticed that a particular issue of his *GQ* magazine featuring Donald Trump on the cover had enjoyed unusually strong sales.[7] He approached Trump about the possibility of writing a book about his business exploits for Newhouse's Random House imprint. It took several meetings to convince Trump, including a mockup cover. Donald liked the cover, but wanted "TRUMP" in larger letters. The allure of the mockup got Donald to "yes."

Next came the hiring of a ghostwriter because Trump would not write the book himself. Tony Schwartz, a journalist with a New York magazine, had published an article portraying Trump as thuggish in his attempt to evict tenants from a new property he owned. Trump loved the article, believing that all publicity was helpful, particularly stories that showed him to be a tough guy in the challenging New York real estate market. He offered Schwartz the ghostwriting job with generous terms: half of the $500,000 advance and half the ensuing royalties.

Trump proved impatient and unresponsive in interviews for the book, so Schwartz instead proposed that he follow Trump around and gather material from his business transactions. For eight months, Schwartz shadowed Trump, even covertly listening in on his business phone calls. As he wrote, Schwartz omitted many unflattering disclosures about Trump and depicted him as a winsome, self-made entrepreneur creatively fashioning deals that were their own satisfaction regardless of the ancillary money and fame they generated. Father Fred figured little in the volume beyond the example he set for his young son. Its most famous passage disputes the harm of bad publicity and espouses embellishment as essential to Trump's way of doing business:

> The funny thing is that even a critical story, which may be hurtful personally, can be very valuable to your business. . . . The final key to the way I promote is bravado. I play to people's fantasies. People may not think big themselves, but they can still get excited by those who do. That's why a little hyperbole never hurts. People want to believe that something is the biggest and the greatest and the most spectacular. I call it truthful hyperbole. It's an innocent form of exaggeration—and a very effective form of promotion.[8]

The book depicts an operating style that remained fixed throughout Trump's career. He ran his own large, privately held business with a small, loyal, and capable staff. His deal making was aggressive and opportunistic. He evidenced an insatiable desire for public attention. Publicity was for him an essential means of generating business, fame, and money. As we will see, his notoriety helped him negotiate some rough business years ahead.

The book sold like hotcakes, spending forty-eight weeks on the *New York Times* bestseller list, and thirteen weeks as number one. Over ensuing decades, it sold over a million copies, earning Schwartz and Trump several million in royalties. Trump aided sales by chasing publicity, appearing on television, and promising to donate half of royalties to charity (still impossible to document today). He now had a taste of the national fame he had so long relished. He even made a surprise trip to New Hampshire, floating the possibility he might run for the 1988 Republican nomination for president. Those political ambitions would soon be suspended because of mounting difficulties brought on by Trump's expansion into enterprises unfamiliar to him and by tumult in his marriage. It's as if he began to believe his own hype.

THE BAD YEARS

Even as *The Art of the Deal* neared publication, business problems began to accrue for Donald Trump. In the early 1980s he began to reach beyond real estate to invest in areas where he had no prior experience. An initial foray involved real estate in Atlantic City, where he planned to build a casino. Obtaining a casino license, he next had to convince the casino company Harrah's to build on his site. Though the construction site he showed them was undeveloped, Trump staged a fake construction operation to convince Harrah's visitors to Atlantic City that the location was a viable one. Trump then worked out an arrangement in which Harrah's financed construction of the hotel and operated it while he provided the license and the land and built the casino/hotel. Trump got half the profits.

The casino hotel opened in spring 1984, under the name Trump Plaza Hotel and Casino. This deal led Trump to pursue the construction of other glitzy new casino hotels in Atlantic City. In early 1985, the Hilton Corporation's newly built casino hotel could not operate because they had been denied a license due to their ties with a supposed mob lawyer. Trump, already holding a license, swooped in and offered to buy the casino. This time Trump put up big money—$320 million—for the purchase and named it the Trump Castle. He bought the place sight unseen, which gave him two comparably sized big casino hotels. Who would run Trump Castle? Trump picked his wife Ivana, who had no experience with such enterprises. Eventually, he hired several experienced casino executives to operate his growing Atlantic City enterprises.

Donald continued his spending spree on gambling enterprises in 1986. His $62 million investment in Bally Manufacturing Corporation, purveyor of gambling equipment, and $70 million in Holiday Inn, parent company of Harrah's, eventually yielded him tidy profits in the tens of millions of dollars. He also spent $29 million for one of the world's largest yachts and ponied up another $8 million to refurbish it. He conspicuously docked it at Atlantic City and used it for private parties for high roller gamblers, though he very seldom frequented it himself.

Trump's most lavish and risky Atlantic City venture was the Trump Taj Mahal, opening in 1988 and financed by $675 million in junk bonds and a personally guaranteed loan from Trump himself. The huge emporium created much debt for both Trump personally and the Trump Organization and helped usher in a major financial reckoning for Donald in 1990.

Donald had engaged in other conspicuous purchases in the 1980s. In 1983 he purchased the New Jersey Generals football team of the upstart United States Football League (USFL) for about $6 million. Trump had no previous experience with sports ownership. Spending freely, he signed several big players to big contracts, pushing other owners to "think big" like he did. His team never won a league championship despite his infusion of cash for players. He encouraged a lawsuit against the National Football League, arguing the established league had violated antitrust law in trying to put the USFL out of business. The USFL won in court but it was a pyrrhic victory. The jury ruled that the NFL was indeed an unlawful monopoly, but awarded the USFL only one dollar in damages. The USFL never took the field again and Trump lost an estimated $22 million on his gaudy foray into professional sports.

Then there was the Trump Shuttle, which he purchased from troubled Eastern Airlines in 1988 for $365 million, a price many industry analysts thought was too high. Trump's inexperience with the enterprise again led him into trouble. He insisted on elaborate furnishings totaling $1 million per plane though customer surveys indicated on-time flights were far more important. His plush carpeting made it difficult for stewardesses to push beverage carts. Distributing free casino chips for his Atlantic City emporiums to Trump Shuttle passengers led to only two being redeemed.

By the late 1980s Trump had begun an affair with model Marla Maples that received abundant coverage in tabloid newspapers. This hurt shuttle business. Shuttle president Bruce Nobles told Trump that women were avoiding his shuttle because of his flagrant womanizing. Nobles argued that "businesswomen in particular are tending to avoid us because they don't like what they're reading about you in the newspaper." Trump laughed and responded: "Yeah, but the guys love it."[9] By 1991, Donald was defaulting on the Shuttle's loan payments. The banks required him to accept US Airways as a buyer. The shuttle never made money. It helped make Trump conspicuous, but this overreach yielded business failure.

Trump's 1980s buying binge also included some substantial real estate items. In 1985 he purchased Mar-a-Lago, the Marjorie Merriweather Post mansion and grounds in Florida for a bargain $10 million dollars and converted it into a private club with expensive membership requirements, a property he owns to this day. In 1988 he purchased the venerable New York Plaza hotel for $50 million and had wife Ivana manage it.

As Trump spent freely on his new casino, gambling, and real estate acquisitions, he also indulged in publicity-generating sports sponsorships. In 1989 and 1990, there was the Tour de Trump bicycle race covering 837 miles and ending at Trump Plaza hotel and casino. He sponsored two World Wrestling Federation "WrestleMania" events at the Atlantic City convention center in 1988 and 1989. His $160,000 got the World Powerboat Championship races moved from Florida to Atlantic City in October 1989, producing havoc for the contestants in the cold choppy Atlantic waters. Trump's fondness for boxer Mike Tyson resulted in a heavyweight championship fight in Atlantic City in June 1988 in which Tyson knocked out challenger Michael Spinks in ninety-one seconds of the first round.

Trump's free spending landed him in big financial trouble by 1990. Banks had loaned many millions to the "whiz kid" author of *The Art of the Deal*, resulting in a massive debt problem for him. Bankers demanded a meeting with him in the spring of 1990 because a $73 million debt payment was due in June. By then, the Trump Organization had accumulated $9 billion in debt. On top of that, Trump had $975 million in personally guaranteed debt. His marriage had crumbled as well, with Ivana wanting a $2 billion divorce settlement.

Donald had big cash flow problems. An economic slowdown had hurt the casino business and the vast new Taj Mahal was incurring debt and cannibalizing customers from other Trump casinos in Atlantic City. His shuttle had lost $34 million in the first half of the year. He sought to sell the shuttle and his huge yacht. The bankers who were meeting with Trump had discovered that he owed them $3.2 billion dollars—a big problem for Trump, but also for the banks.

Trump's celebrity, which had mounted considerably in the last few years, proved to be a big asset in addressing his debts. Trump's close friend Howard Lorber explained the value of Trump's celebrity in the situation: "His name was on everything. That was a concern. If you have an asset and part of it is the Trump name, what good is it to tarnish the name? Why beat him up? It became self-serving to work it out so that you don't tarnish the name. That was the big advantage he had—having that brand name was terrific."[10]

So all those Trump properties were given an extended lease on life by the bankers, but Donald had to accept some stringent terms. The bankers provided $65 million and delayed interest payments on approximately $1 billion in loans for five years. They placed liens on his house, personal aircraft, yacht, Mar-a-Lago and three casinos. They even put him on a personal spending leash, starting at $450,000 a month and declining within two years to $300,000. The high limits would allow Trump to keep up appearances to maintain the value of his celebrity branded properties. As he signed the agreements, he handed out copies of the latest account of his personal business adventures, a book titled *Surviving at the Top*. Donald eventually sold the shuttle, yacht, and Plaza Hotel to address his vast debts. Bankruptcies followed for the Taj Mahal in 1991 and the Plaza and Castle casinos and New York Plaza Hotel in 1992. These were Chapter 11 bankruptcies, which kept partial Trump ownership and the Trump name on the properties.

Donald's affair with Marla Maples and divorce battle with Ivana had attracted much media attention during his financial slide. In 1990, the tabloid *New York Post* at one point put his affair and divorce on its front page for eight days in a row and the *New York Daily News* had him on its front page for twelve consecutive days. When Ivana got wind of Donald's financial problems, she dropped her divorce demand to the prenuptial agreement's $25 million and accepted that in the divorce settlement.

Donald's 1993 marriage to his mistress since 1989, Marla Maples, featured Trumpian glitz. Over one thousand guests attended the nuptials at New York's Plaza Hotel in 1993, which Trump finally sold in 1995. Marla and Donald had a daughter, Tiffany, in 1993.

A GRADUAL ASCENT TO PEAK CELEBRITY

The decade of the 1990s was a slow financial crawl for Donald Trump as he worked through his massive debt problems. His flamboyance and chronic desire for public attention had contributed to his free spending binge in the late 1980s. Trump would find more financially prudent ways to stay in the public eye after his financial reversals. The casinos, however, remained a long-term debt problem for him and his organization until he took them public in 1995. Trump also refocused on real estate opportunities that would aid his financial recuperation.

By 1993, he claimed to have reduced his personal debt from $975 million to $115 million. Yet he and his organization ran out of money and he had Nick Ribis, head of the Trump Organization, call Donald's siblings for a cash bailout. He needed $10 million to stay afloat. Brother Donald received the funds from them in return for a guarantee that he would repay them. Then in 1994, he asked for another $20 million more and they again came through for him. According to Alan Marcus, a Trump advisor at the time, Donald this time agreed that repayment would eventually come, if necessary, from the $35 million he had inherited from his father's estate.

The borrowing from the family got Trump through the financial difficulties, though he later denied any such borrowing had occurred. The end of a recession improved the casinos' cash flow, but the public corporation containing the casinos lost money every year from 1995 to 2005. In 1995, he offered public shares in them, raising $2 billion that largely went to retire his personal and his organization's debt. By mid-1995, he touted that he was debt-free.

Throughout his career, the net worth of Donald Trump's financial empire has never been very reliably estimated. Trump has always claimed his net worth in the billions, but *Forbes* magazine dropped him from its "billionaire" list in 1990 in the midst of his financial difficulties. He did return to the list a few years later, but his claimed net worth was always much higher than that assessed by *Forbes*. Throughout this time, Trump regularly lobbied the magazine for a higher place on its "wealthiest" list. By 2018 he ranked #259 on their list with a net worth of $3.1 billion, far below the $10 billion net worth he claimed during the 2016 campaign.

Trump returned to the original source of his wealth—New York City real estate—with several projects in the 1990s. In 1994 he created the Trump International Hotel and Tower by purchasing the Gulf and Western building on Columbus Circle. In 1996, the Bank of Manhattan Trust building became the Trump Building at 40 Wall Street. At Riverside South he began a multiple building development in 1997 that he called Trump Place. From 1994 to 2002 he held a 50 percent share in the Empire State Building. In 2001 he completed Trump World Tower. In 2004, the Hotel Delmonico became Trump Park Avenue, a collection of luxury condominiums.

Trump had less success with his far-flung resort business, employing Chapter 11 bankruptcies in 2004 and 2009. His golf courses in the United States proved profitable, but not those overseas.

Throughout the 1990s, Trump kept his name in the public eye by associating himself with a variety of flashy activities. From 1996 to 2015, he was part or total owner of the Miss Universe pageants, encompassing also the Miss USA and Miss Teen USA pageants. Some pageant contestants later complained that Trump entered their dressing rooms when they were not fully clothed and that he engaged in nonconsensual kissing with some contestants over the years. He bragged about the physical attributes of contestants during his regular appearances on the Howard Stern radio show, which began in 1993 and lasted until 2013. The talk was raunchy, involving ratings of women's physical attributes and discussion of possible sex acts with them.

Trump allegedly discovered that his wife Marla Maples, who had developed a "party girl" reputation, had been found alone with a male bodyguard on a beach near Mar-a-Lago at 4 a.m. one morning in 1996. They separated the following year, a few days short of the deadline for a generous prenuptial agreement to begin. Divorce occurred in 1999 with Maples eventually accepting—for Trump—a relatively modest $2 million settlement. Marla settled in California where she raised daughter Tiffany.

While separated, Trump met Slovenia-born model Melania Knauss at the Kit Kat nightclub on Times Square in 1998. A relationship blossomed. She appeared on the Howard Stern radio show with him in 1999 and campaigned for him when he sought the Reform Party presidential nomination in 2000. An engagement followed in 2004 and marriage on January 22, 2005—her first, his third—with a lavish reception following at Mar-a-Lago. Their son Barron arrived in 2006, Trump's fifth child from his three marriages.

Trump's big media breakthrough occurred in 2003, when television producer Mark Burnett approached Trump about hosting the first season of a reality program titled *The Apprentice*. The show would pit two teams of contestants in competitive situations undertaking projects with various businesses. At the end of each program, Trump would decide which of the contestants would be removed from the competition. At first wary, Trump eventually agreed to do it with an initial compensation of $50,000 per episode and half ownership in the show. The climactic scene of each episode was filmed in the dark, wood paneled boardroom of the Trump Organization.

The show was a big hit, ranking number seven in total audience in its first season. The producers immediately discovered that Trump performed well on television and increased his presence in subsequent episodes. In its first three seasons the program garnered eight Emmy nominations but won no Emmy awards. Though Trump exaggerated its ratings as being the best overall, over most of its seasons it did rank in the top twenty in total audience ratings. In season seven, the format was recast as *The Celebrity Apprentice* in which celebrities from the worlds of radio, television, music, sports, and other backgrounds competed in order to win money for their favorite charities. Ratings were middling when Trump left the show in 2015 as he considered a presidential run.

The program portrayed Trump as a billionaire with superb business instincts and abilities, the very personification of success. He introduced each episode with characteristic exaggeration: "I'm the largest real estate developer in New York. I own buildings all over the place. Model agencies, the Miss Universe pageant, jetliners, golf courses, casinos, and private resorts like Mar-a-Lago. . . . I've mastered the art of the deal and have turned the name Trump into the highest-quality brand. And as the master, I want to pass along some of my knowledge to somebody else." In fact, Trump has never ranked as the largest New York real estate developer by financial volume, though he frequently made that claim.

Millions of Americans encountered this portrayal over the show's fifteen seasons. His signature line at the conclusion of each episode— "You're fired"—became a national catchphrase. Trump had grasped a higher celebrity profile than ever before. He loved it, and proceeded to expand the presence of his personal "brand" across American commerce and culture. As he told a second season contestant: "all publicity is good publicity. . . . When people get tired of you is when you do more publicity, because that's when you become an icon."[11] He thought that goal was in sight.

Donald Trump energetically pursued it in the wake of the first season of *The Apprentice*. He appeared on Don Imus's syndicated radio show every week for a year and a half and continued his occasional Howard Stern radio visits. Two-minute radio commentaries featuring Trump celebrity gossip were on the air from 2004 to 2006. In 2004, he hosted *Saturday Night Live* and was the subject of a Friar's Club roast. In 2005, an overalls-clad Trump sang "Green Acres" with actress Megan Mullally at the 2005 Emmy awards. He regularly spoke at "success seminars" for a hefty fee. A steady stream of books by Trump and ghostwriters appeared. After 2000, the focus of the books shifted from the personal business memoirs of his first three volumes. Now he dispensed advice on how to succeed in business and life and offered many political pronouncements. Fourteen books listing Trump as a coauthor and one with him a sole author with an uncredited ghostwriter appeared between 2000 and 2015.

Trump's well-established pugnacity appeared frequently in his books and radio appearances. His 2007 volume *Think Big: Make It Happen in Business and Life*, coauthored with Bill Zanker, features a contentedly belligerent Trump. In recounting his ongoing, nasty spat with actress Rosie O'Donnell, he proclaims: "That is why I tell people, 'get even!' This is not your typical advice, get even, but this is real life advice. If you don't get even, you are just a schmuck!" His approach derived from a harsh worldview: "The world is a vicious, brutal place. It's a place where people are looking to kill you, if not physically, then mentally. . . . You have to know how to defend yourself. People will be nasty and try to kill you just for sport. Even your friends are out to get you!"[12]

He showcased his pugnacity in a series of antics at World Wrestling Federation matches in 2007. Donald engaged in a staged feud with Vince McMahon, WWF founder, in a "Battle of the Billionaires." In January, he had real paper bills of actual cash rain over the crowd like confetti. Trump had initially proposed an actual wrestling match with McMahon, but eventually settled for sponsoring rivals in a match during "Wrestlemania 23"— with the losing sponsor having his head shaved bald by the winner. At the event at which this deal was signed, Trump pushed McMahon over a table in the ring. McMahon in turn refused to shake Trump's hand and poked him in the shoulder, so Trump slapped McMahon in the face. At a March 5 appearance, Trump knocked McMahon down and crawled across the floor to whack him again. Trump's wrestler won the match, allowing him to shave McMahon's head at center ring right before a howling crowd. This extended Trump's "brand" to a new portion of the national audience.

Trump energetically built his celebrity and wealth through licensing in the wake of his television stardom. This showcased his name across the economy. By merely licensing his name he was not responsible for the business practices of the companies employing his licensed name. The total number of licensing deals exceeded fifty, but many of them concerned products that failed to sell. The list includes a dizzying array of items and services, among them Trump steaks, vodka, wine, board games, magazine, mortgage company, financial services company, men's wear, mattresses, coffee pods, lamps, wall sconces, and a GoTrump travel search engine. He licensed his name to a resort and golf course in Indonesia, a hotel in Toronto, and private mansions in the United Arab Emirates.

A particularly controversial licensing arrangement involved Trump University, a "real estate training program" operated by the Trump Organization from 2005 to 2010. It did not offer college credit, but rather videotaped and live "training" on how to be a successful real estate investor. The university also licensed a "Trump Institute" owned and operated by Floridians Irene and Mike Milin, which also offered real estate training. Trump received payments from the institute but did not control its operation. The university charged between $1,500 and $35,000 for its training programs and attracted a total of 7,611 participants during its operation. Donald Trump only appeared via brief videotapes.

The university attracted three lawsuits for illegal business practices. Participants had complained about high-pressure tactics from university employees to buy more expensive training programs. As the suits proceeded, a deposition from Trump became public in which he indicated he had never met the instructors of the program, contradicting its advertising that he had handpicked them. On November 18, 2016, Trump, in the midst of a presidential transition, retired the lawsuits by agreeing to a $25 million settlement. He claimed he would have won the suits but wanted to end them because of his forthcoming presidential duties.

During the 2016 primary campaign, Trump had publicly complained about US District judge Gonzalo Curiel, then presiding over a suit in the case. Trump complained that Curiel was a "Mexican" and should recuse himself. Curiel had been born in Indiana, the son of Mexican immigrants. In June 2016, Trump released a statement indicating he did not intend to disparage the judge's ethnicity but rather his rulings in the case. By then, Trump's long-simmering political ambitions were bearing fruit as he barreled toward the GOP presidential nomination.

TRUMP'S PATH INTO POLITICS

Trump's 2016 candidacy capped a long flirtation with presidential politics that had begun decades before. During an early peak in his celebrity, following the success of *The Art of the Deal*, Trump demonstrated presidential aspirations. Trump's public relations employee Dan Klores convinced Trump to take out full-page ads in four national newspapers attacking US foreign policy. Klores then told reporters Trump was considering running for president on the 1988 GOP ticket and arranged for him to visit New Hampshire, site of the first presidential primary. Trump made the trip but eventually abjured running. Klores later described it as a very effective form of book promotion. Trump later recommended himself as a good running mate for Republican nominee George Herbert Walker Bush.

Trump's next presidential foray occurred in 1999. On October 8, during one of his several appearances on CNN's Larry King Live interview show, Trump announced he was leaving the GOP to join the Reform Party and forming an exploratory committee to run for president. Roger Stone, a controversial former Republican political operative, became his campaign advisor. Trump's inexperience with national issues surfaced in a subsequent *Meet the Press* interview with veteran journalist Tim Russert. January 2000 saw publication of Trump's first political book, *The America We Deserve*, followed by a visit to Minnesota to confer with Independence Party Governor Jesse Ventura. On February 19 he dropped out of the race, indicating he might not be able to win as a nominee of an internally divided third party. He nevertheless remained on the Reform Party ballot in the Michigan and California primaries and won them both.

One year later, Trump hosted a fundraiser for New York Senate candidate Hillary Clinton at Trump Tower. Trump then was a registered independent but was demonstrating remarkably flexible political views, believing it was important to get along with major New York politicians. Accordingly, he contributed $4,700 to Clinton's campaigns from 2002 to 2009, and joined the Democratic Party in 2001. That year, he endorsed the strong liberal Fernando Ferrer in the New York City Democratic may-oral primary. Trump then supported the equally liberal primary winner Mark Green, who lost to then-Republican Michael Bloomberg.

Trump proved pragmatic with his political money and support in the years before he ran for president. He contributed to New York Democrats but said he voted Republican for president in 2000, 2004, 2008, and 2012. His party registration changed seven times between 1999 and 2012. By that year, his celebrity status had earned him a place among the GOP frontrunners. He was among the top candidates in national GOP opinion polls and was the polling favorite among arch-conservative Tea Party supporters.

The billionaire's attacks on President Obama were sensational and controversial. He condemned the president's healthcare reform, the Affordable Care Act, as a job killer. Trump began a public campaign to cast doubt on Obama's American birth—perhaps instead he was born in Kenya and ineligible for the presidency. As Trump was about to embark on an exploratory visit to New Hampshire, Obama released his Hawai-ian birth certificate. At the 2011 White House Correspondents Dinner, attended by Trump, Obama ridiculed the billionaire: "no one is happier to put this birth certificate matter to rest than The Donald. And that's because he can finally get back to focusing on the issues that matter—like, did we fake the moon landing?" (April 30, 2011) The audience roared while Trump's visage registered chagrin.

Decades as a celebrity helped Trump rank second in the 2012 nomi-nation preference polls to Mitt Romney, but Trump again declined to run. Trump endorsed Romney in early February, recorded endorsement calls for him and attacked Obama on Twitter, which had now become a favorite venue for the billionaire. Trump offered Obama $5 million for a charity of the president's choosing if he released his college transcripts and passport information. Obama did not deign to reply to the offer.

The billionaire kept himself in the public eye in preparation for a pos-sible presidential run. From April 2011 to his June 2015 announcement of his presidential candidacy, he appeared weekly on a "Mondays with

Trump" segment of the Fox News morning show "Fox and Friends." This came about because his prior occasional appearances on Fox had garnered big audiences. Fox News would provide much assistance to his 2016 presidential campaign. The network carried many of his 2015 and 2016 rallies live. Trump made himself available for interviews with the network whenever he could.

EXPLAINING TRUMP'S CELEBRITY SUCCESS

The first master analyst of political rhetoric, Aristotle, provides the best summary judgment on Trump, the celebrity candidate. The billionaire's campaign was short on policy detail and realism but overflowing with hyperbole. Two thousand four hundred years ago, Aristotle explained the power of hyperbole. Hyperbolic overstatements often work rhetorically because they "show vehemence of character. And besides, the emotional speaker always makes the audience feel with him, even when there is nothing in his arguments; which is why many speakers try to overwhelm their audience by mere noise."[13]

Trump in business, on the campaign trail, and in the White House constantly sought to overwhelm rivals and audiences with noise. Though never a majority-approval president, he has been able to maintain his core support over the years through his rhetorical methods, limiting the effectiveness of those who quarrel with his often dubious evidentiary claims. Why? "The effects of fact-checkers or analysts who identify the lack of substance or the fallacies in the rhetoric are nullified among those with whom Trump's rhetoric resonates because the hyperbole, by definition, is an exaggeration not meant to be taken literally."[14]

Journalist Selena Zito noted that the media takes Trump literally but not seriously and his supporters take him seriously but not literally. So despite Trump's deserved reputation as the scourge of media fact-checkers, he continues to find a large, appreciative audience. Years of living in the limelight helped him develop a persona and rhetoric that brought him to political preeminence. Lots of Americans in 2016 detested politics as usual and longed for an "authentic" outsider who would speak his mind and offer a striking alternative to the governmental status quo. Trump had been speaking his mind constantly for forty years, assembling a louche but blunt personal brand. That struck enough Americans as sufficiently insurgent and authentic to land him in the White House.

The four most frequent words in candidate Trump's 2016 tweets were, in rank order, "Trump," "great," "Donald," "America." A lifetime of celebrity branding empowered those words.

4

TRUMP'S 2016 BREAKTHROUGHS

When Donald and Melania Trump descended the escalator at Trump Tower on June 16, 2015, he was about to embark on a presidential campaign that showcased the four characteristics of his forty-year crusade for celebrity. First, his ongoing desire for constant attention would be satisfied readily by the spotlight of a presidential campaign. In addition to his continual media availability, the candidate published a book on America's problems, *Crippled America*, ghostwritten predominantly in the first person. Second, Trump would insist on having personal control over the campaign's direction through the presidential primaries. His initial campaign director, Corey Lewandowski, adopted "Let Trump Be Trump" as the effort's informal slogan. Trump would guide the effort based on his "instincts," much as he had guided his celebrity career. Third, the candidate would engage in unconventional and attention-getting antics, from harsh Twitter attacks on rivals to debate boasts about his sexual prowess and endorsements of his licensed product line after primary victories. Fourth, his penchant for exaggeration and false statements would appear throughout his candidacy.

Trump's campaign organization from early 2015 to the summer of 2016 was limited to a small central staff. Its main functions were event planning of his big rallies and arranging his media appearances. The campaign was initially funded by the candidate himself, who could legally spend unlimited funds on behalf of his candidacy and sported a modest budget up to the GOP convention. During the primaries, the campaign did no polling of its own and its policy research was limited. The campaign paid less for ads than was usual for a candidate of his stature. This was a benefit of his celebrity career, which now produced extensive coverage of events and candidate pronouncements.

Lewandowski initially scheduled Trump for house visits to small groups in New Hampshire but the crowds they encountered were so large that Trump suggested they schedule large rallies instead. Thus a media sensation was born. Cable news outlets carried the rallies live throughout much of the election year. Trump also made himself freely available for media interviews. The explosion of Trump coverage amounted to a huge in-kind contribution to his campaign, courtesy of the networks that themselves enjoyed high ratings from the Trump media onslaught.

The Trump campaign's small staff, frenetic schedule and demanding boss eventually led to an exhausted Lewandowsky and his June 20 firing as campaign manager. His successor, Paul Manafort, ran afoul of the candidate by trying to manage his media appearances. Trump insisted on doing that himself. Manafort resigned on August 19, replaced by Steve Bannon and Kellyanne Conway as campaign managers. For the fall campaign, Conway and Tony Fabrizio did polling. Veteran Trump employee Brad Parscale, first hired in 2011, directed the campaign's impressive digital media operation throughout 2016.

Trump contributed $66 million of his own funds for his 2016 campaign and overall spent $647 million compared to his general election rival Hillary Clinton's expenditure of $1.2 billion. The "Trump show," however, produced astounding levels of free media coverage. Political scientist Peter Francia estimates the worth of Trump's free media at $4,960,000,000 compared to Clinton's $3,200,000,000.[1]

What made the rallies so newsworthy? "In simple terms, a Trump rally is a dramatic enactment of a particular version of America. Or, rather, it enacts how Trump and his followers would like America to be. In a phrase, it is an identity festival that embodies a politics of hope."[2] At the center of the show stood a man who knew how to attract attention and wow sympathizers with direct, unvarnished, and memorable language. His presentation was that of a "celebrity outsider" speaking informally and candidly, fed up with politics as usual:

> "We've got a lot of problems. We've got a lot of problems. That's right, we don't win anymore. . . . We don't win anymore. We're going to win a lot—if I get elected, we're going to win a lot. (Applause) We're going to win so much—we're going to win a lot. We're going to win a lot. We're going to win so much you're all going to get sick and tired of winning. You're going to say oh no, not again. I'm only kidding. You never get tired of winning, right? Never." (Hilton Head, South Carolina January 20, 2016)

Trump condemned special interest money, saying he didn't need it because of his wealth. The billionaire bluntly attacked rival candidates, criticized foreign policy deal making that he promised he would improve, guaranteed a tall wall on the Mexican border that Mexico would pay for and complained that the people in his audience had been forgotten by the power holders in Washington: "And the people want results. They're tired of it. They're tired. The politicians talk, and you know a lot of times I'll give a speech, I'll say how to fix a solution because nobody's gonna be better at bringing jobs back than me, nobody. Nobody's even close. [Audience cheers] And I'm not going to be affected by people that gave me money because I've turned down tens of millions of dollars. I feel, like, so stupid for doing that" (Pittsburgh, Pennsylvania April 13, 2016).

The bellicose Trump was on bold display throughout the 2016 campaign. He proved gifted at describing opponents with catchy epithets, a sort of insult comedy: "Lyin' Ted" (Ted Cruz), "Little Marco" (Marco Rubio), "Low Energy" Jeb Bush and "Crooked" Hillary. The verbal brickbats reaped constant media attention and entertained many of his supporters. Trump's tweets also kept him at the center of media coverage. By July he had 10,267,655 twitter followers compared to Hillary Clinton's 7,765,519. The billionaire's tweets were frequently caustic. A recurrent target was the media and its reports of his exaggerations and prevarications: "@CNN is so negative it is impossible to watch. Terrible panel, angry haters" (April 19, 2016), "The media is so dishonest. If I make a statement, they twist it and turn it to make it sound bad or foolish. They think the public is stupid" (July 20, 2016).

His rivals caught it regularly on twitter: "Hillary said 'I really deplore the tone and inflammatory rhetoric of his campaign.' I deplore the death and destruction she caused—stupidity" (December 23, 2015). "Jeb's new slogan—'Jeb can fix it.' I never thought of Jeb as a crook! Stupid message, the word 'fix' is not a good one to use in politics!" (November 1, 2015). "Lyin' Ted Cruz steals foreign policy from me, and lines from Michael Douglas— just another dishonest politician"(March 23, 2016).

He'd included verbal sallies on policy, too: "Russia has more warheads than ever, North Korea is testing nukes, and Iran got a sweetheart deal to keep theirs. Thanks, @HillaryClinton" (September 26, 2016). "We're going to cut taxes BIG LEAGUE for the middle class. She's raising your taxes and I'm lowering your taxes!" (October 9, 2016)." MY PRO-GROWTH Econ Plan: ✓Eliminate excessive regulations! ✓Lean government! ✓Lower taxes!" (October 9, 2016).

Trump employed his practiced attention-getting skills in candidate debates, where he was contentious, blunt and newsworthy. In response to a prior Rubio insinuation about the size of Trump's hands and what that might imply about his genitals, Trump in debate replied by holding up his hands to the camera: "Are they small hands? He referred to my hands. If they are small, something else must be small. I guarantee you, there is no problem." (March 4, 2016). He launched harsh debate attacks on Hillary Clinton, claiming she was a "typical politician. All talk, no action. Sounds good, doesn't work. Never going to happen. Our country is suffering because people like Secretary Clinton have made such bad decisions in terms of our jobs and in terms of what's going on" (September 26, 2016).

Trump's long celebrity career prepared him to grab and keep the limelight better than any presidential candidate before him. He had planned ahead for 2016, copyrighting his memorable campaign slogan,

"Make America Great Again" in 2012. His availability was constant, his verbal wordplay catchy, and for those inclined to support him, rousing and thoroughly enjoyable. He played himself, not some politician from Washington. He had perfected that act since the 1970s, mastering the art of personal hype. The result was vast media attention and one of the stunning upsets of American political history.

RELYING ON THE MEDIA

On June 16, 2015, Donald Trump stepped on to the golden elevator at Trump Tower on his way to the main lobby. In the lobby he was greeted by dozens of supporters (as well as paid actors and confused tourists) and a large number of reporters. Trump, a real estate magnate and reality TV celebrity, stood before an awaiting podium and announced that he would seek the Republican nomination for president. Trump had considered the idea of running for president in the past, but never actually ran. Given these prior flirtations, many observers wondered if Trump was really serious about running or if he was more interested in the publicity generated by a run. Trump joined an already crowded field of candidates, most of whom had prior experience running for or holding elective office. At the time of his announcement, it was unclear just how Trump would distinguish himself from the other, more experienced, candidates.

Trump's announcement speech was long and at times meandering. His actual declaration that he was running came fifteen minutes into the speech. Though many wondered if they should take his candidacy seriously, Trump used the speech to introduce many of the key issues, and accompanying controversies, that came to define his campaign. Trump remarked that there was an unprecedented crowd of people present for his announcement and said that the crowd was beyond anyone's expectations. Within days of the announcement it was discovered that the Trump campaign had issued a casting call and paid actors $50 to attend the speech.[3]

The announcement covered a host of policy issues. On trade, Trump sounded now familiar claims that countries such as China, Japan, and Mexico were taking advantage of the United States because of bad trade deals. He dismissed the Affordable Care Act as "useless" and a "disaster." He pledged to repeal it and replace it with something much better. Trump touted his deal-making abilities and promised to bring jobs and manufacturing back to America. He criticized the cost of the Iraq War as well as the Iran Nuclear Deal negotiated under President Obama. Perhaps the most memorable and controversial part of his announcement was his focus on illegal immigration. According to Trump, illegal immigrants from Mexico are "people that have lots of problems, and they are bringing those problems to us. They are bringing drugs, and bringing crime, and their rapists."[4] In response, he promised to build "a great wall at the Southern border" that Mexico would pay for.[5]

Trump's controversial comments about Mexican immigrants generated considerable media coverage and discussion of his campaign announcement. This came to be a familiar pattern during Trump's candidacy and beyond—controversial remarks would result in extensive coverage, often producing the media exclusion of other candidates or officeholders. It's clear that this was exactly what Trump wanted. In his book *The Art of the Deal*, Trump wrote, "If you are a little different, or a little outrageous, or if you do things that are bold or controversial, the press is going to write about you." To Trump, all publicity is good publicity. And he knew how to generate it. Although Trump was and is a frequent and fierce critic of the news media, having declared the press "the enemy of the people" on multiple occasions, he likely owes his successful nomination run to the press and media coverage of his campaign.

Given his frequent and often scathing assessments of the national press, it may seem odd to suggest that Trump owes much of the credit for his rise from reality TV star to president to the press. But it's hard to imagine a nominee Trump, let alone, a President Trump without giving some credit to frequent, and, yes, even favorable, coverage that Trump received upon announcing his candidacy in the summer of 2015 and effectively securing the Republican nomination in May 2016.

Political scientists refer to the months leading up to the first presidential primary or caucus as the "invisible primary." It's a period during which potential candidates compete to secure money, endorsements, staff commitments and, perhaps most importantly, press coverage. Simply stated, media exposure can boost a candidate's standing in public opinion polls, and improved standing in polls can bolster a candidate's ability to secure endorsements and raise money. Trump coupled traditional media coverage with an unprecedented use of social media, which often generated even more traditional media coverage, to propel himself to the Republican nomination and then to the presidency.

Prior to the Trump candidacy, there was a conventional wisdom that endorsements and money were key to a candidate's early success. From that success, a candidate might expect rising poll numbers, and with rising poll numbers would come more media coverage. Likewise, any mistakes or controversies might derail a campaign. The press is a crucial player during the invisible primary. Prior to the early 1970s it was political party power brokers or party bosses who played the role of filtering out weaker candidates and promoting stronger candidates. As discussed in chapter 2, parties have largely surrendered that role and in recent decades that screening process has fallen mostly to the press. Most voters learn about politics and candidates secondhand, via the news, so media coverage is crucial to a candidate's success or failure.

The media has traditionally served as an arbiter of what a candidate can say without paying a political price. Donald Trump routinely pushed the boundaries of acceptable candidate behavior and survived. In November 2015, Trump mocked Serge Kovaleski, a journalist who suffers from arthrogryposis, a condition that affects the movement of joints and is noticeable in his hands and arms. Trump mimicked Kovaleski by waving his arms around while holding his hands at an unusual angle. To any reasonable observer it was clear that Trump was mocking the journalist's condition. In response to the outrage that followed, Trump denied having mocked the reporter. Despite clear video evidence, Trump's polling numbers were unaffected.

That same month, Trump proposed "a total and complete shutdown of Muslims entering the United States" following a terrorist attack in Paris. The remarks were criticized by civil liberties advocates as well as fellow Republicans. In July 2015, Trump ridiculed Senator John McCain. McCain had spent five years in a Vietnamese prisoner of war camp. Trump referred to McCain as a "dummy" and said McCain was "a war hero because he was captured. . . . I like people who weren't captured."[6] Perhaps the most significant controversy came in the closing weeks of the general election. In an audio recording from a 2005 Trump appearance on an episode of *Access Hollywood*, Trump bragged about a prior effort to have an affair with a married woman and said that as a celebrity, women let him do anything he wishes, including grabbing their genitalia.[7] Though the national press, and his political opponents, routinely condemned Trump for his offensive and inflammatory comments and tweets, he paid no apparent political price. Rather than harm Trump's campaign, the increased coverage boosted his campaign. Trump was able to use social media, especially Twitter, to bypass traditional media and connect with voters.

During the 2015 invisible primary Donald Trump received far more media coverage than any of his Republican rivals and the coverage that he received was actually overwhelmingly positive or neutral, a combination of coverage defined as favorable. This coverage advantage appears to have violated two long-standing norms of invisible primary media coverage. One, poll standing tends to determine how much media coverage a candidate receives and two, press coverage during this phase is typically focused on a candidate's fundraising prowess. During the invisible primary, however, former Florida Governor Jeb Bush was atop the polls and had raised far more money than any other potential Republican candidate. Donald Trump barely registered in the polls and had raised no money. Yet, Trump received twice the amount of media coverage than did Bush.[8]

This coverage translated into millions of dollars in free media exposure and most certainly bolstered his campaign and contributed to his steady rise in opinion polls. Beyond receiving more coverage than his potential rivals, Trump received more favorable coverage.

Trump benefited from the fact that journalists are attracted "to the new, the unusual, the sensational."[9] Trump had argued much the same in *The Art of the Deal* and was a perfect candidate to exploit that attraction and became perhaps "the first bona fide media-created presidential nominee."[10] *New York Times* columnist Nicholas Kristof echoed that sentiment, writing "we in the news media gave Trump $1.9 billion in free publicity in this presidential cycle. That's 190 times as much as he paid for in advertising, and it's far more than any other candidate received."[11] Kristof's observation does not negate the fact that Trump was able to tap into an underlying current of discontent and voter anger. Rather it suggests that without the media, Trump's lack of a political constituency and credible claims to the presidency may have prevented him from making that connection with the electorate.

It may be hard to believe that most of Trump's media coverage was favorable during the crucial months of the invisible primary, but that largely resulted from the narratives typically employed by the press during the early stages of a campaign. Early coverage is mostly focused on the horse race aspect of the campaign. A candidate's position in the horse race typically fits into one of four possible storylines. A candidate may be leading, gaining ground, losing ground, or trailing. As one might imagine, stories about candidates leading or gaining ground tend to be more favorable as they focus on those things going well within the campaign. Likewise, stories about a candidate trailing or losing tend to be unfavorable as the focus is often on those aspects of the campaign that are going wrong.[12] This horse race approach to coverage benefited Trump and hurt Jeb Bush, the assumed frontrunner.

As a result of the free media coverage afforded Trump, his poll numbers began to rise. So stories written about the Trump candidacy often focused on his rise from a candidate with no real support to that of a real contender. A poll released at the end of July 2015 found Trump atop the GOP field. Trump was the first choice of 20 percent of Republicans. Jeb Bush, the former frontrunner, had fallen to 10 percent.[13] As a result, Jeb Bush found himself on the losing ground end of coverage as stories focused on the failure of his endorsements, fundraising, or poll position to secure the nomination.

It's important to note that nearly all the coverage of Trump during this stage focused on the horse race and very little focused on his personal characteristics or policy issues.[14] It merits mention that most of Hillary Clinton's invisible primary coverage was negative as she engaged in an unexpectedly close contest with Bernie Sanders. She was losing ground. Though Trump had the highest negatives of any Republican candidate and fared worse in potential 2016 matchups, he was gaining ground— connecting with Republican voters.

By the time of the first primary in January 2016, Trump had established himself as the clear frontrunner with a double-digit lead over the closest challenger. As a result, Trump's domination of media coverage continued throughout the primary season. Trump's string of primary victories and rising delegate count resulted in favorable coverage, still fixated on the horserace, until the very last month of the primary season and after all his potential opponents had dropped out of the race. This was driven by the dynamic of Trump as the unconventional candidate who was gaining ground or leading.

Perhaps more surprising, Trump continued to receive more media coverage than Clinton or Bernie Sanders even after the Republican nomination battle was essentially over. But the tone of the coverage changed. In the final month of primary contests, with all challengers vanquished, Trump's coverage went from 53 to 47 percent positive in the preceding months to 61 to 39 percent unfavorable in the closing weeks. Why the change? With the nomination all but secured, stories about the horserace became less common. More coverage focused on Trump's personality and his issue positions. Those horserace stories that did appear tended to focus on him trailing Clinton or Sanders in the general election. In short, coverage of Trump did not turn negative until attention shifted away from the Republican primary horse race and to the 2016 general election.[15]

Trump endured only a brief period during which his nomination was in doubt. Though Trump dominated the polls and the primaries, he had never topped 50 percent of the vote in GOP primaries and continued to poll below 50 percent in national polls. Though Trump was the clear leader in the count of delegates needed to secure the Republican nomination, by early April it was not clear that Trump would be able to secure the 1,237 delegates needed to win the nomination on the first ballot at the Republican convention. This led to speculation over a brokered convention or backroom deals designed to deny Trump the nomination.

In response, Trump started railing against what he labeled a corrupt, rigged, and phony system that was being used to deny the nomination to the person with the most votes and delegates—him.[16] This was a populist message tailor-made for voters angry with the establishment. It's important to note that 2016's other populist insurgent, Bernie Sanders, had similarly accused the Democratic Party of rigging the system to deny him the nomination.[17] Trump went on to clear 50 percent in the New York primary and in every subsequent primary. By the time of the Republican convention Trump had more than secured the delegates needed to win the party nomination.

Trump would return to his claims of a rigged system in his general election contest with Clinton. As polls continued to show him trailing Clinton, Trump made ever more references to the rigged and crooked system and a dishonest media that was working to deny him, and his supporters, the presidency.[18] It proved to be an effective strategy for keeping his supporters engaged and motivated. The claims were controversial and unprecedented from a major party nominee, but Trump had long ago learned that controversy guarantees coverage. Additionally, his claims of a rigged system echoed the accusations made by Bernie Sanders and may have encouraged some of them to support Trump or a third-party candidate. At the very least it may have undermined their willingness to support Clinton and encouraged some to simply sit out the election.

It's certainly possible that Trump won in spite of his boorish behavior, but it's worth considering as well that he won in part because of it. Research has shown that voters tend to react positively to candidates who communicate in a more informal way. Compared to his Republican opponents and to Hillary Clinton, Donald Trump made more use of nonstandard and low-complexity words and made much greater use of Twitter (considered to be a less formal form of communication). According to linguist Jennifer Sclafani, who spent two years studying Trump, his communication style was crucial to his success and he connected with many voters because he communicates the way that they do.[19] Unlike most politicians or presidents, Trump does not speak in a manner that conveys a greater level of education or refinement than his audience. His tendency to use simple two- or three-word phrases, a casual tone, repetition, and hyperbole—even his frequent midsentence topic changes—reflect things that people do in everyday speech. Trump clearly recognized that he was connecting with voters when he remarked during a February 2017 news conference, "That's how I won . . . I won with news conferences and probably speeches. I certainly didn't win by people listening to you people, that's for sure."[20]

TRUMP'S WIN IN HISTORICAL CONTEXT

Beyond the exit polling and popular discontent detailed in chapter 1 and the media coverage detailed earlier, history is also instructive as to the reasons for Trump's victory. It is extremely rare for voters to follow a two-term president by electing a candidate from that president's party. George H. W. Bush in 1988 is the only recent example. So Hillary Clinton suffered the same fate as most post-incumbent partisans, including Adlai Stevenson in 1952, Richard Nixon in 1960, Al Gore in 2000, and John McCain in 2008. It's no wonder then that election prediction models developed by economists and political scientists and based on so-called fundamental factors such as economic growth, consumer confidence, and incumbent approval rating painted a picture of the 2016 election outcome that was far less certain than those predictions based almost entirely on public opinion polls.

In September 2016, results from nine such models set to be featured in the journal *PS: Political Science and Politics* were released, and they revealed no consensus regarding who would win, let alone what the margin of victory would be. Tellingly, those models based more on historic fundamentals such as economic conditions or incumbent approval tended to see a rosier picture for Donald Trump. Models that relied more on contemporary public opinion polls painted a better picture for Hillary Clinton. All told, existing predictive models and a review of American presidential elections pointed to a very close election and one where the incumbent party would face disadvantages.

But these *fundamentals* were often overshadowed by the larger than life major party candidates vying for the presidency. Trump's lack of qualifications, unorthodox style, and frequent tendency to say or do offensive things compared poorly to Hillary Clinton's extensive résumé and measured tone. The stark contrast created the impression of an election outcome that was easier to predict.

It's difficult to estimate the effect, individually or combined, of the myriad factors that may have contributed to the outcome. There can be no doubt but that Russian agents interfered in the election. Less clear is whether that interference substantively affected the outcome. It's clear that Russian hackers were successful in breaching the email servers of the Democratic National Committee as well as the email account of Clinton campaign chief John Podesta. They were effective as well at hyping the contents of hacked emails. But there's no evidence that the Russians breached any election systems or interfered with the actual vote. The investigation conducted by Robert Mueller concluded that there was no collusion between any member of the Trump campaign and any Russian agents.

Though the steady drip of leaked emails may have contributed to voters' lack of trust in Clinton and further stoked voter anger, there were serious missteps taken by the candidate and campaign as well. The FBI investigation into Clinton's use of a private and unsecured email server while secretary of state was a controversy of Clinton's own making. Bill Clinton's impromptu private meeting with Attorney General Loretta Lynch, in the midst of that investigation, when their planes crossed paths at a Phoenix airport, certainly did not help either.

Though Hillary Clinton clearly believes that James Comey's decision to reopen the investigation into her email server just ten days prior to the election was crucial to understanding her loss, a panel of polling experts convened to understand how pollsters got the election wrong concluded the evidence of a Comey effect was "mixed" at best.[21] Another counterpoint to Comey is that Clinton's lead over Trump in the polls was already declining in the days before the Comey announcement. The decline began following a widely covered announcement of substantial premium increases under the Affordable Care Act. As detailed in chapter 1, Trump tapped in to much of the populist anger and resentment that fueled the Tea Party movement in 2009 and 2010. The creation of the Affordable Care Act played a leading role in that movement. The rising premiums, which mostly impacted the self-employed, fed the narrative of a federal government that was not on the side of working- or middle-class Americans.

Some have suggested that the Libertarian Candidate Gary Johnson and Green Party Candidate Jill Stein may have cost Clinton the election, but this is a rather specious claim. As a limited government Libertarian, it's reasonable to conclude that Johnson drew more votes from Trump than from Clinton. Jill Stein may have appealed to more progressive voters turned off by Clinton's connections to the establishment. In Michigan, Pennsylvania, and Wisconsin there were just enough Stein votes that a reallocation of nearly every Stein vote to Clinton would have changed the outcome. But a study by political scientists Christopher Devine and Kyle Kopko raises serious doubts about the validity of simply reassigning Stein's voters to Clinton. Their analysis of exit polling data in those three key states determined that Stein's absence from the race may have delivered Michigan to Clinton, but not Wisconsin or Pennsylvania. Pennsylvania and Wisconsin would have been tied with Clinton and Trump having a fifty-fifty chance of winning each. But even this analysis likely overstates Stein's impact as it assumes that her supporters would've shown up on Election Day had she not been on the ballot.[22]

THE DEMOGRAPHIC KEYS TO TRUMP'S VICTORY

In their 2002 book *The Emerging Democratic Majority*, John Judis and Ruy Teixeira theorized that Democrats were on the verge of establishing a lock on the Electoral College. Democrats were strongest in the "postindustrial" sections of the country where the production of ideas had replaced manufacturing. Republicans were strongest in the regions where the transition to postindustrialism had lagged. Judis and Teixeira argued this new majority was driven by demographic changes taking place in growing metropolitan regions that would serve as the breeding ground of the new Democratic majority. The key to the emerging Democratic majority was demography. The key metropolitan regions were home to the growing minority and professional populations essential to Democrats. As argued by the authors, this emerging majority included another crucial member—the white working class. Though these former members of the Democratic coalition had abandoned the party for Ronald Reagan, they increasingly came to share the values of their professional counterparts. As such "Republican appeals to race (or resentment against immigrants), guns, and abortion have largely fallen on deaf ears, and these voters have not only rejected Republican social conservatism, but also reverted to their prior preference for Democratic economics."[23]

The 2006 midterm elections, followed by Barack Obama's comfortable victory in 2008, convinced many that the Democratic majority had indeed emerged. The substantial Republican victories in 2010 raised serious doubts about the demographics as destiny theory of the emerging Democratic majority. Following Barack Obama's reelection in 2012, Ruy

Teixeira argued that the election result vindicated the arguments presented in the emerging Democratic majority and suggested that said majority may be here to stay, but only if Democrats embraced and pursued the activist government progressive legacy of the 1960s. Then came 2014 and the culmination of the Republican gains made in Congress, statehouses, and state legislatures during Obama's tenure. Teixeira's co-author, John Judis, revisited the emerging majority thesis in 2015 and concluded that their theory was flawed, perhaps fatally. Not only had white working-class voters continued their decades-long migration to the Republican party, but middle-class whites were joining them in the journey. More troubling for the theory was the fact that middle-class Hispanics and young voters were less Democratic than had been predicted as well.

In the 2016 election, Trump's victory revealed many flaws in the emerging majority thesis. According to exit polls Donald Trump won an overwhelming majority of white working-class voters. In the key battleground states (and central bricks in Clinton's "Blue Wall") of Pennsylvania, Ohio, Michigan, and Wisconsin, Trump saw the Republican margin of victory among white working-class voters grow from twelve points in 2012 to thirty points in 2016. Perhaps crucial to Trump's victory were the defections to Trump by white voters who had voted for Obama in 2012 and those defections were considerable. Clinton received support from only 74 percent of white voters who had previously voted for Obama. Breaking the data down a bit further reveals that Clinton received only 78 percent of such voters with less than a bachelor's degree. Her support was even lower in the Rust Belt states that delivered the election to Trump. Clinton was harmed as well by a decline in turnout among black voters and an increased turnout by noncollege-educated white voters. Compared to 2012, there was a larger share of black registered voters who did not vote in 2016 and a smaller share of white registered voters without a college degree.[24]

But the emerging Democratic majority included more than just white working-class voters, and even among those other voting blocs Trump defied expectations. He carried college-educated whites as well as suburban voters which Judis and Teixeira viewed as a crucial component of the emerging Democratic majority. Trump received the support of 61 percent of white working-class women and split the vote of married women with Clinton. Though he lost black and Hispanic women by wide margins, he did better among those groups against Clinton than had Mitt Romney against Obama in 2012. Trump performed better among Hispanic voters in general than had Mitt Romney. Among young voters, Clinton's nineteen-point advantage over Trump was decidedly smaller than Obama's twenty-three-point advantage in 2012 or his thirty-four-point advantage in 2008.

It's important to understand that a reliance on demographics, in an electoral system driven more by geography, misses a crucial element of the 2016 outcome. The emerging Democratic majority was very much premised on demographics as key Democratic constituencies grew in strength and number in major metropolitan areas. By their very numbers they would come to dominate American politics and elect Democrats. The flaw in the theory was laid bare in a multipart analysis conducted by Sean Trende and David Byler for the popular RealClearPolitcs website.[25] Simply stated, if the Democrats' greatest strength is demographic, then the GOP's greatest strength is geographic. The Democratic Party's coalition is poorly distributed throughout the United States. It is overwhelmingly concentrated in large metropolitan regions and this limits the party's ability to win presidential elections.

In 2016 Hillary Clinton won the largest metropolitan areas by a historic margin of thirty points and that margin in highly populated areas certainly contributed to her three million popular vote win. But these large metropolitan areas are mostly located in already Democratic, non-swing states. So her margins added to her popular vote total, but not her Electoral Vote total. Clinton not only lost but performed worse than any recent Democrat in small cities and towns and in rural America. In swing states like Florida, there are more than enough votes in those areas to offset an advantage in the large metropolitan regions. In 2000, Al Gore won the popular vote by 550,000 votes and lost the election by an agonizingly close four electoral votes. Much like Clinton, Gore won in the largest metropolitan areas and lost in small cities and towns and in rural America.

But the gap between his vote share in the largest metropolitan regions as compared to rural America was approximately eighteen percentage points. Hillary Clinton won the popular vote by three million votes but lost the election by a decidedly not close seventy-two electoral votes. The gap between her support in large metropolitan areas and rural America was thirty-two percentage points![26]

In some respects, Clinton inherited a Democratic Party dominated by voters from increasingly progressive urban areas. As such, the party has tailored its message and policy agenda to maximize support from those areas but at the expense of a growing number of voters, especially white working-class and middle-class suburban voters. Equally as important as the flawed demographic assumptions made by Judis and Teixeira were their expectations about support for activist government. On Election Day 2016 nearly 70 percent of voters said that they were dissatisfied or angry with the federal government and by a 50–45 percent margin voters said that government is doing too much as opposed to too little. By a three-to-one margin voters wanted the next president to be more conservative than Barack Obama as opposed to more liberal.

Such views serve to fuel a right-wing populism that sees government as a detriment to the success of working- and middle-class people. Both Donald Trump and Hillary Clinton were historically unpopular and a majority of voters considered Trump to be unqualified for the presidency, but Trump was the candidate that better reflected voter attitudes regarding government. The concentrated nature of the Democratic coalition, and the tailoring of the party's message to progressive and urban voters not only contributed to Trump's victory, it impeded the Democrats in Senate and House races.

THE LIMITS OF TRUMP'S LESS THAN IMPRESSIVE WIN

It's important to note that though Trump's victory was unexpected, it was not necessarily very impressive in a historical context. Trump was the weakest post-incumbent challenger in two hundred years. Including 2016 there have been a total of seventeen presidential elections in which no incumbent was on the ballot following the reelection of an incumbent. In the prior sixteen post-incumbent elections there was a very clear trend in both the popular (state and national) and electoral vote, a significant shift of votes to the party that was out of power. How significant a swing? Across the prior sixteen post-incumbent elections that average vote swing toward the party out of power was ten percentage points. If the analysis is narrowed to only those post-incumbent elections to have occurred after the Civil War the swing is six percentage points in the popular vote. Barack Obama won the popular vote by 3.9 percentage points with 51.1 percent to Romney's 47.2 percent of the vote. In a hypothetical post-incumbent election in 2016, history would suggest that that a six-point shift would deliver 45.1 percent to the Democrat and 53.2 percent to the Republican. Hillary Clinton outperformed the historical pattern, receiving 48.2 percent of the vote and Trump underperformed with 46.1 percent. Trump also ran poorly compared to other Republicans on the ballot. Republican candidates for the House of Representatives won the popular vote by nearly 1.4 million votes, receiving 49.1 percent of the vote to Trump's 46.1 percent. Trump trailed the Republican Senate candidates in most of the states with a contested race.[27]

Trump's underperformance relative to other post-incumbent challengers coupled with Clinton's overperformance suggests that Trump's flaws as a candidate were a drag on his campaign. Revelations in an *Access Hollywood* tape of Trump bragging that his star power allowed him to grope women and that he tried very hard to initiate an affair with a married woman almost certainly harmed his campaign and limited his ability to attract voters. Trump's frequent attacks on women's appearance and the multiple accusation that he had sexually harassed women were harmful as well.

Trump won by winning three of the four states that were decided by less than one percentage point—Michigan, New Hampshire, Pennsylvania, and Wisconsin. Trump carried Michigan, Pennsylvania, and

Wisconsin by a combined seventy-seven thousand votes. A shift of thirty-eight thousand votes from Trump to Clinton in those three states would have delivered the presidency to Clinton. The race was just that close for Clinton and history suggests that it should not have been. With every presidential election there is a tendency among scholars and pundits to ask whether or not the outcome had resulted in a dramatic political reordering. There is reason to conclude that the 2016 shock to the system was a rather predictable outcome given political history since the late 1960s.

But clearly there were limits to Trump's appeal. Though Trump won, he lost the popular vote by three million votes. As president, his approval rating has been mired in negative territory. His inflammatory rhetoric has added a new intensity to America's already polarized politics. Offensive statements made about immigrants, women, members of Congress, judges, and others have created difficulties for him in reaching out to members of his own party, let alone attempting to build bridges with the Democrats who regained control of the House of Representatives in the 2018 midterm elections. Congressional Democrats who may otherwise be open to working with Trump on matters such as infrastructure face the possibility of open revolt by the base of their party. The most active members of that base formed a "resistance" movement dedicated to blocking Trump and his agenda. Even a majority of Republicans believe that Trump is undermining his agenda with his rhetoric.

Trump has returned to his 2016 campaign tactics repeatedly during his first term. Under unified Republican control he would rail against failed Republican leadership to explain his frustrated agenda. Following the 2018 election, Trump blamed what he called the "Do Nothing" Democratic House. Trump and his defenders routinely accuse the media of being biased and argue that his low polling numbers are fake. In response to the government whistleblower report that prompted the House impeachment inquiry, Trump and his team have blamed a "Deep State" conspiracy consisting of partisan bureaucrats working to oust the president. It remains to be seen if the tactics that secured him the Republican nomination, and ultimately the presidency, will work again in 2020.

5

PRESIDENT TRUMP

The turbulent path of the Trump presidency could be foretold by his aggressive personality showcased over his years as a media celebrity. Beyond all the surface conflict, though, what did Trump promise to achieve as president? As his reelection campaign arrives, what has he delivered? Chapters 5 and 6 sort through these questions.

Trump's top 2016 issues are readily evident from his often spontaneous campaign talks. Here's the list:

Shake up established ways of Washington government and politics

Build a border wall, enhance immigration enforcement, and reform immigration laws

Call out the "fake news" media and hold them to account

Appoint conservative judges

Cut taxes, spending, and regulations, and balance the federal budget

Create an "America First" foreign policy—employ aggressive trade policy, rethink current military alliances, rewrite or withdraw from international agreements, and employ presidential unpredictability as a tactical asset

Did Trump deliver? What were the reasons for his successes and failures with this basket of promises? A lot of that depended on how Trump's personality fared in the White House environment. His fiery personality produced constant drama that became a trademark of his presidency.

THE OFFICE AND THE MAN

When Donald Trump walked into the White House on January 20, 2016, he entered the top of a large executive branch organization, far more entrenched and extensive than his privately held real estate business. He now had authority not only over the presidential office but the vast executive branch of national government detailed in chapter 1.

This is a vast management challenge, far greater and more complex than Donald Trump's personal business enterprises. Trump also has to contend with an imposing list of presidential leadership roles that all modern presidents since Franklin Roosevelt (1932–1945) have undertaken. Clinton Rossiter enumerated these back in 1956: leader of the executive branch, Congress, public opinion, armed forces, international leader of free nations, and ceremonial head of state.[1]

That is a lot to unpack and for any one president to undertake. Then there's the matter of the president's personality. It affects presidential decisions, media coverage and the ongoing operation of the many parts of America's presidency. What sort of personality did Trump bring to this boatload of responsibilities?

Trump's traits closely resemble those of "dominator" presidents, so classified by psychologists Steven Rubenzer and Thomas Faschingbauer in their landmark study of presidential personality. The dominators of presidential history were Andrew Jackson, Lyndon Johnson, and Richard Nixon. "They were exceptionally bossy, demanding, domineering, manipulative; none was even tempered. All acted assertively, were self-centered and egotistical, stubborn and hardheaded and thought highly of themselves."[2] Trump seems to share many of these traits. He has installed a portrait of Andrew Jackson, whom he admires, in the White House.

How might a dominator like Trump govern? His dominator predecessors all ranked low on personal character, high in neuroticism and very low on openness and agreeableness. Since Trump shares these characteristics, his presidency has proved to be a jarring ride.

Trump's aggressiveness and frequent tweets have produced many controversies over the truthfulness of his assertions. The media challenges many of his statements as factually untruthful. The *Washington Post*'s fact checking has identified over ten thousand instances of "false and misleading claims" from his inauguration to June 10, 2019—10,796 claims in 869 days. Many of his tweets—limited to 280 characters—and public statements "lack context." Examples abound. One is a June 5, 2017, tweet in which he refers to his immigration executive order as a "TRAVEL BAN" despite the fact that his administration previously had stated that the order was not a travel ban. On May 10, 2019, he tweeted "We have lost 500 Billion Dollars a year, for many years, on Crazy Trade with China. NO MORE!" In fact, the 2018 annual trade deficit with China was $378 billion. Further, who loses from a mutually profitable exchange between citizens of two countries that aggregates into a trade deficit?

Trump's embellishments of the factual record have long been part of his approach in business. Given the nation's polarized politics, not everyone views Trump's exaggerations as innocent. The low agreeableness and character of the dominator loom in such behavior, producing a bumpy path for Donald Trump in the White House.

A TURBULENT TRANSITION TO THE PRESIDENCY

There were many bumps along the way for Trump from Election Day on November 8 to his inauguration on January 20, 2017. Trump's loss of the popular vote by a 2.1 percentage point margin while winning the Electoral College ignited considerable public controversy. Democratic "blue America" responded with outrage, public demonstrations, demands for recounts, legal challenges to Trump electors, and pleas to Trump state electors to disregard their state's popular vote when electing the next president.

Actual transition planning had begun months earlier than Election Day, but that process was turbulent. On May 6, 2016, the candidate announced that New Jersey Governor Chris Christie, a rival for the GOP nomination who later endorsed Trump, would head the transition effort. By October, the transition staff numbered over one hundred and included many policy experts added to compensate for a dearth of them on the campaign staff.

But on November 11, Trump instigated a big shakeup of the transition staff. He ousted Chris Christie and many of his transition subordinates, apparently dissatisfied with the pace of the transition and Christie's involvement in the "Bridgegate" corruption scandal in his home state. The change was abrupt, with the Christie-appointed staffers quickly shown the exit and in one case at least, locked out of the transition office. Vice president–elect Pence took over supervision of the transition.

MANY APPOINTMENTS, MUCH TURNOVER

Trump's top appointees proved to be varied in background, but less demographically diverse than those of his predecessor, Barack Obama. Trump's cabinet initially included only three women—Betsy DeVos at Education, Elaine Chao at Transportation (Secretary of Labor under George W. Bush and spouse of Senate Majority Leader Mitch McConnell), and UN Ambassador Nicki Haley. Trump's rival for the 2016 GOP nomination, physician Ben Carson, became the only African American in the cabinet as Secretary of Housing and Urban Development. Alexander Acosta, Dean of Florida International University law school, became the first Latino member of Trump's cabinet as Secretary of Labor.

Retired generals initially populated Trump's national security team. Trump's reliance on the generals reflected his stout praise of the US military during the 2016 campaign, an allegiance probably born of his happy years as a teenage student at New York Military Academy.

Defense Secretary James Mattis, a retired four-star Army general and former commander of the US Central Command, directed US forces in the Middle East from 2010 to 2013. Mattis encountered foreign policy disagreements with Trump and left under contentious circumstances in December 2018 to be replaced by Patrick Shanahan and later Mark Esper, both former executives with defense contractors. A retired four-star Marine Corps general, Homeland Security Secretary John Kelly, had headed the US Southern Command from 2012 to 2016. Kelly eventually succeeded Reince Priebus as White House Chief of Staff and served in that capacity for sixteen months.

National Security Advisor H. R. McMaster, a retired three-star Army general, pioneered innovative battlefield tactics during the Iraq War. McMaster soon wore out his welcome by presenting Trump with lengthy written memos that the president did not want to read. He resigned in April 2018, replaced by John Bolton, a renowned hawk and former UN Ambassador during the second Bush presidency. Trump reportedly told Bolton at the time of his appointment "You're not going to try to talk me into another war, are you?"[3] Apparently weary of Bolton's hawkish advice, Trump accepted Bolton's resignation on September 10, 2019. He was replaced by veteran hostage negotiator Robert O'Brien.

Before McMaster, a particularly controversial appointment was three-star general Mike Flynn as the president's National Security Advisor. Flynn had endorsed and campaigned for Trump after being fired as head of the Defense Intelligence Agency under Obama. Flynn was dismissed by Trump in mid-February after Vice President Pence asserted that Flynn had failed to disclose important information about Flynn's meeting with the Russian ambassador in Washington.

Appointment as Director of National Intelligence went to former GOP Senator Dan Coats of Indiana. The director sits on the president's cabinet and National Security Council. Trump reportedly grew tired of his stark intelligence assessments and Coats resigned on July 28, 2019. Representative Mike Pompeo of California received appointment to the important non-Cabinet post of CIA Director. Pompeo moved up to Secretary of State in April 2018. He was replaced at the CIA by Gina Cheri Haspel, herself a CIA veteran.

Trump's diplomatic appointments brought far less relevant experience to their new jobs than did the generals. Secretary of State Rex Tillerson, like Trump, had no prior governmental experience. He began a lengthy career in international business as an engineer and rose to become chief executive officer of the Exxon international corporation. UN Ambassador Nicki Haley was in her second term as South Carolina Governor when appointed to her position, which carries cabinet rank. Both departed office after relatively short tenures in those jobs.

During his presidency's first year, Trump was very much the dominant voice of his administration's foreign policy. Secretary of State Tillerson kept an unusually low profile in the early months of the administration. The president often took the initiative in stating major themes of his foreign policy in speeches both domestic and overseas and, of course, in his evening tweets. At times he contradicted the policy statements of UN Ambassadors Haley and Tillerson. The initial Trump budget proposed severe cuts in the State Department budget while significantly boosting military spending. Trump fired Tillerson in March 2018, publicly referring to him as a "blockhead." He was replaced by CIA Director Mike Pompeo, with whom Trump has expressed more confidence.

In contrast to Trump's populist pronouncements on the campaign stump, his economic policy appointees hailed from Wall Street and the conservative Washington establishment. Treasury Secretary Steve Mnuchin worked for Goldman Sachs for seventeen years and later for other New York Investment firms. Commerce Secretary Wilbur Ross was founder and president of the W.L. Ross and Company investment firm. Investment Banker Gary Cohn became the president's chief economic advisor and chair of his National Economic Council. Cohn resigned in

April 2018, to be replaced by Larry Kudlow, a Reagan administration economic official and prominent talking head on cable television. Chair of the president's Council of Economic Advisors, Kevin Hasset, came from the American Enterprise Institute, a beltway think tank populated by many establishment conservatives. Another conventional Washington nominee was David Shulkin as Secretary of Veterans Affairs. Shulkin had served as Undersecretary of Health in that department in the Obama administration. Trump fired Shulkin in March 2018 amidst allegations of unethical actions during an overseas trip. He was replaced by Robert Wilkie, a former Defense Department official.

Three members of Congress also entered the Trump cabinet. Montana Representative Ryan Zinke became the first Montanan to serve as Interior Secretary. Physician and Georgia Representative Tom Price took charge of the massive Department of Health and Human Services, the department with the largest annual budget. Both Zinke and Price resigned due to ethics controversies, replaced by Alex M. Azar II, a former drug company executive, at Health and Human Services and David Bernhardt at Interior in an "acting" capacity. Senator Jeff Sessions of Alabama, the first Senator to endorse Trump's 2016 candidacy, took the reins of the Department of Justice as attorney general.

Trump's "justice agenda" coincided with Jeff Sessions's priorities, auguring new restrictions on immigration, more aggressive immigration enforcement, and a steady stream of conservative judicial nominees. Sessions, however, received many public complaints from the president about his appointment of Robert Mueller as Special Council to investigate Trump's campaign's possible collusion with Russia during the 2016 campaign. Sessions resigned, much to Trump's satisfaction, the day after the 2018 midterm elections. William Barr, attorney general during the first Bush presidency, replaced Sessions.

Three other cabinet appointees had considerable governmental experience, if not Washington experience. Energy Secretary Rick Perry had served two terms as GOP governor of Texas. As a 2016 presidential candidate, he had called for the abolition of the department, but recanted that position upon receiving nomination to the post. Sonny Purdue, former Republican governor of Georgia, became Secretary of Agriculture. Oklahoma Attorney General Scott Pruitt was named head of the Environmental Protection Agency, a regulatory body he had frequently criticized and litigated against in court on behalf of his state. Pruitt resigned in 2018 amid multiple ethics controversies and was replaced by Andrew Wheeler, who formerly provided legal representation for the coal industry. Most domestic cabinet secretaries proved to be lower profile figures during the administration's first months, reflecting their departmental agendas' reduced standing among the administration's priorities.

"YOU ARE FIRED" AND FEW ARE HIRED

What did this constant churn and change of personnel reveal about Trump as president? A Brookings Institution review of his appointments found that by August 2019, 75 percent of his top appointees had left the administration and that 33 percent of the positions had turned over more than once, an unusually high rate of change.[4] As chief executive of his private firm, Trump quickly removed employees who dissatisfied him. He did the same as president. A host of his initial appointees either resigned or were fired, many voicing frustration with Trump's impetuous executive style.

The administration proved very slow in making lower-level executive branch appointments. Trump the outsider lacked an established network of Washington allies who could suggest nominees and facilitate their administration approval. Trump's transition had also been slow off the mark, further delaying nominations. Laggard nominations blunted the impact of the "Trump revolution" in Washington by missing the available momentum during his early months in the White House. Frequent turnover also plagued subcabinet appointments. By June 2019, several subcabinet positions remained occupied by individuals in an "acting" capacity without permanent appointment, among them the Federal Aviation Administration, Food and Drug Administration, Equal Employment

Opportunity Commission, Occupational Safety and Health Administration, Immigration and Customs Enforcement, Federal Emergency Management Agency, and Secret Service.

TRUMP'S CHANGING WHITE HOUSE STAFF

A major locus of media-centered drama during Trump's presidency has been the turmoil surrounding the operations of his White House staff. Though Reince Priebus, 2016 national GOP party chair, became White House chief of staff, it quickly became clear that Trump would operate independently in communicating with the public—often by smartphone tweets—and pursuing his personal presidential agenda. Trump in effect became a media freelancer within his own administration. He's continued this approach throughout his presidency so far.

Trump daily granted presidential access to a wide variety of staff people. His oval office is often populated by many underlings, in marked contrast to the more introverted Obama, who kept the office quiet and access to it tightly regulated by his chief of staff.

Trump's volatile temperament, in combination with the loose organizational structure of his White House, led to an atmosphere of fear, spawning many leaks from his staff. Initially, this led to a steady stream of media stories as Priebus, senior counselor Steve Bannon, counselor Kellyanne Conway, daughter Ivanka and her husband, and senior advisor Jared Kushner, were portrayed as constantly jockeying for position. Bannon, never comfortable in his staff position, left the administration in August 2017. The jockeying continued when Priebus was replaced by Homeland Security Secretary John Kelly as chief of staff and when Kelly resigned at 2018's end to be followed by OMB Director Nick Mulvaney in that position. This gave Mulvaney a unique position as both OMB director and acting White House chief of staff.

The "who's up, who's down" media stories provided an annoying distraction for the administration. Trump's first press secretary, Sean

Spicer, formerly the press spokesperson for the Republican National Committee, was a particular target of rumors. Spicer had the toughest job in Washington. At times the press office would provide a rationale for an administration action only to have that rationale contradicted by a presidential tweet. The White House shifted from "no drama Obama" to "constant drama Trump."

The challenges facing the White House press office crested during a Trump-generated administration crisis, the firing of FBI Director James Comey. Spicer and his Deputy Press Secretary Sarah Huckabee Sanders initially stated that the president had "no choice" but to fire Comey based on a memo written by Deputy Attorney General Rod Rosenstein. According to Spicer, the firing was really Rosenstein's doing. Shortly afterward Trump in an interview contradicted them, claiming that he had long intended to fire Comey "regardless" of what the Justice Department recommended, terming Comey a "showboat" and "grandstander."

In July 2017, Spicer resigned upon learning that Anthony Scaramucci, nicknamed "Mooch," a Wall Street investor with no experience in media relations, would become his boss as White House director of communications. Scaramucci's 250-hour tenure in the position ended when his profanity-laden interview with journalist Ryan Lizza led to his dismissal by the new Chief of Staff John Kelly. Longtime Trump aide Hope Hicks took over as acting director in August 2017 and served as director from September to the end of March 2018. Hicks was determinedly low key in contrast to the bombastic Mooch. Trump then retreated further into his media comfort zone by naming Bill Shine, onetime co-president of the Fox News Channel and Fox Business Network, as communications director. Shine resigned in March 2019.

Spicer was succeeded by his Deputy Press Secretary Sarah Huckabee Sanders. Sanders, the daughter of former Arkansas governor and Trump backer Mike Huckabee, found her new job just as challenging as her predecessor. She spent much of her time with reporters defending the president's controversial tweets and factually dubious assertions. Sanders resigned in June 2019 and was replaced by former Trump campaign aide Stephanie Gresham, who became both communications director and White House press secretary.

Trump kept the White House atmosphere charged through his treatment of his staff associates." Trump prefers a management style in which even compliments can come laced with a bite, and where enduring snubs and belittling jokes, even in public, is part of the job" according to the *Washington Post*.[5] This "dominator" behavior is remarkably similar to that of Lyndon Johnson, who frequently scorned his staff, at times meeting with an aide while sitting on the toilet.[6] Having one's staff scampering like scared rabbits has its costs for a president. Fear of your boss can prevent important but unwelcome information from coming his way and promotes unhelpful leaks. Both problems seem likely to persist in Trump's White House.

ETHICS QUESTIONS SURROUNDING TRUMP

Another unusual aspect of the Trump presidency is its handling of ethics questions. During the 2016 campaign, candidate Trump made several promises to clean up the Washington "swamp." His "Contract with the American Voter" included promises to place a five-year ban on White House and Congressional officials becoming lobbyists, a lifetime ban on White House officials lobbying for foreign governments, and a complete ban on foreign lobbyists raising money for US elections. Several such reforms would be included in the "Clean up Corruption in Washington" act that he would submit to Congress. It has yet to become a Trump administration priority.

Candidate Trump nevertheless received criticism regarding several ethics issues arising from his distinctive financial position and holdings. His uniqueness was defined by his net worth, which he claimed was $10 billion during the campaign but was estimated at $3.5 billion in 2017 by *Forbes*. How does a person with such extensive financial holdings prevent his investments from influencing his presidential decisions? Walter Schaub, Director of the Office of Governmental Ethics, argued that nothing short of total divestiture would erase the ethical concerns created by Trump's wealth.

Trump would have none of that. He instead agreed to give up his position as an officer of the Trump Organization, pledging no communication with it beyond regular receipt of profit and loss statements. His sons, Donald Jr. and Eric, along with company executive Alan Weisselberg, would take over management of the organization. The president-elect also canceled all pending international deals with his organization. Schaub and other ethics experts termed Trump's approach totally inadequate. Several noted that the arrangement would not prevent Trump from knowing his businesses' source of revenue or even block him from receiving income from the trust. Might foreign governments try to curry favor with Trump by staying at his hotels?

The Democratic Attorneys General of Maryland and the District of Columbia brought suit in federal courts arguing that Trump's arrangement violated the Constitution's "emoluments clause." Article I Section 9 Clause 8 states in part, "no Person holding any Office of Profit or Trust under them, shall, without the Consent of the Congress, accept of any present, Emolument, Office, or Title, of any kind whatever, from any King, Prince, or foreign State." Two lawsuits were filed claiming that because of his continuing business interests, Trump is violating the foreign emoluments clause of the Constitution. The Fourth Circuit Court of Appeals threw out the case as based on "speculative" evidence, though a similar suit filed by Democratic Members of Congress still proceeded in federal district court.

Trump as candidate and president has not released his income tax returns, making him the first candidate to not release them since 1976. Trump's refusal also was a personal change of course. In 2012, Trump called on GOP presidential nominee Mitt Romney to release his tax returns and in 2015 indicated he would release his tax returns. Then repeatedly in early 2016, the candidate indicated that he would release his tax returns as soon as the audit they were undergoing was completed. This remains his current position.

Democrats have launched several efforts to force disclosure of Trump's taxes, including a 2019 subpoena for them from House Ways and Means Committee chair Richard Neal (D-MA). The Democratic New York state government passed a law allowing Congress access to Trump's state tax returns and the California state government created a law denying candidates access to their 2020 ballot unless they release their tax returns. The Trump administration filed legal challenges and these controversies ended up in federal court.

Trump's nondisclosure is particularly striking give the breadth and complexity of his financial holdings. Disclosure would provide a field day for inquisitive journalists. It might also clarify the financial ethics of the president and perhaps quiet his critics on the issue.

Though President Trump promised strong ethics standards in his administration, he engendered controversy by granting "ethics wavers" to seventeen White House staff members, including four former lobbyists. To "drain the swamp" of Washington, Trump prohibited senior officials hired into the executive branch from working on "particular" government matters that involve their former clients or employers for two years. Yet he waived that prohibition for some top employees. In addition, a "blanket waiver" was granted to all White House staff communicating with the media, including former Breitbart media head Steve Bannon. The exemptions granted by Trump were unusually speedy and numerous. Obama granted only seventeen such waivers during his eight years in office.

The Trump administration's unusual ethics arrangements call into doubt his promise to "drain the swamp" in Washington. Trump, however, did attempt to follow through on two ethics promises. On January 28, 2017, he issued an executive order that required that new executive branch employees pledge that they would not lobby the particular agency they worked at within five years of the end of their employment there. The order further required new appointees to agree to a lifetime ban on lobbying for a foreign government. Waivers can be issued for this order, however. The administration has appointed dozens of former lobbyists to work for the agencies that they sought to influence. The tensions already evident between Trump's roles as international businessperson and government reformer will loom throughout his time at 1600 Pennsylvania Avenue.

Ethics questions reached crisis level for Trump in the fall of 2019 when House Speaker Pelosi (D-CA) instructed several chamber committees to begin impeachment investigations of the president. The triggering event was a whistleblower report from a CIA operative at the White House about a July 25 phone call between Trump and the president of Ukraine, Volodymyr Zelensky. During the call, Trump stated that "there's a lot of talk about Biden's son, that Biden stopped the prosecution and a lot of people want to find out about that so whatever you can do with the Attorney General would be great. Biden went around bragging that he stopped the prosecution so if you can look into it. . . . It sounds horrible to me." At the time of the call, President Trump was withholding nearly $400 million in military aid from Ukraine. Democrats seized on this as unethical "quid pro quo" pressure to enlist a foreign government to find "dirt" on a political opponent. Some GOP Trump defenders found the words troubling and others saw it as a legitimate presidential attempt to root out corruption. House Democrats' support for an impeachment investigation mounted, making Trump the fourth president—joining Andrew Johnson, Richard Nixon, and Bill Clinton—to be subject to an impeachment inquiry.

TRUMP AND RUSSIA: THE NEVER ENDING STORY

Trump's ethics controversies initially received far less media attention than the ongoing revelations and investigation into the relationships of the Trump campaign and administration with the Russian government. From the evening of his surprise election victory on November 8, the topic of Trump and his campaign's relations with the Russian government and diplomats has seldom been far from the headlines. The controversy has several themes.

First, what exactly was the role of Russian hackers and the Russian government in the 2016 US election? Second, what relationships existed between Russian hackers, businesses and the Russian government and Trump's campaign and transition staff and presidential administration? Third, what contact did Trump himself have with Russians during the campaign and since his inauguration? It's important to note that the constant stream of media stories about Trump and Russia included many from "unnamed sources" whose reliability was unclear. Some of the stories later turned out to be false or publicly unverified.

The context for these controversies begins with public disclosure of thousands of damaging emails by the Hillary Clinton campaign during the summer and fall of the 2016 campaign. The CIA later stated that Russian officials, at the direction of President Putin, had given the emails to the WikiLeaks organization which then publicized the stolen electronic correspondence. The embarrassing disclosures certainly did not help the Clinton campaign. Other later media reports indicated that Russian military intelligence sent phishing emails to one hundred local US election officials before the 2016 voting.

On August 14, 2016, Trump campaign chair Paul Manafort resigned in the wake of a *New York Times* report that he had received $12.7 million in undisclosed payments from a pro-Russian political party in Ukraine. Manafort denied the allegations.

A major controversy erupted for the new Trump administration on February 13, 2017, when National Security Advisor Mike Flynn resigned amid allegations that he made improper overtures to Russian Ambassador Sergey Kislyak before Trump took office. The firing offense, however, was that he had misled Vice President Pence on the nature of those contacts. FBI Director James Comey at a Congressional hearing on March 20 confirmed that an active FBI investigation was examining links between the Russian government and Trump associates as part of a broader investigation of Russian interference in the election.

On May 9, Trump fired James Comey, creating great public controversy about the dismissal and the reasons for it. The firing was peremptory and surprised Washington. Reports then surfaced that Trump asked Comey in a private meeting to end an investigation into fired National Security Advisor Mike Flynn's ties with Russia. Comey himself had initiated some of these leaks. This raised the specter of a possible obstruction of justice by Trump in attempting to abort an ongoing FBI investigation. The president, however, has legal authority to fire an FBI director and to direct him in his duties.

On May 17, a week after Comey's firing, Deputy Attorney General Ron Rosenstein appointed a special counsel with broad authority to investigate Russian influence in the 2016 election, Trump campaign, and Trump administration. Robert Mueller, former FBI director with a reputation for integrity, took charge of the investigation as special counsel. He was empowered to issue subpoenas and to recommend charges, though criminal charges cannot be filed against a current president. Trump responded—as he would many subsequent times—that he was the target of a "witch hunt" by his political opponents.

Mueller's lengthy investigation did yield indictments of thirty-four people and three Russian businesses on charges ranging from financial crimes to computer hacking. These included Paul Manafort and Richard Gates for illegal lobbying activities prior to his joining the Trump campaign. Campaign associates Roger Stone, George Papadopoulos, and former Trump lawyer Michael Cohen were charged with lying to prosecutors during the investigation.

In his final report delivered in late March 2019, Mueller stated his investigation "did not establish that members of the Trump Campaign conspired or coordinated with the Russian government in its election interference activities."[7] The president had fulminated to staff and the public about the Mueller investigation and at times had ordered his staff to fire Mueller, yet the administration ultimately took no actions to impede his investigation. Did Trump's action constitute obstruction of justice? Mueller stated that his investigation ultimately came to "no conclusion—one way or another" on whether Trump's actions had obstructed justice, which left the Attorney General William Barr with the task of determining "whether the conduct described in the report constitutes a crime."

To Mueller, the evidence was "not sufficient" to establish that Trump had obstructed justice. Mueller concluded, a bit ambiguously, "While this report does not conclude that the President committed a crime, it also does not exonerate him." Attorney General Barr found inadequate grounds for an obstruction indictment, stating that the White House "fully cooperated with the Special Counsel's investigation, providing unfettered access to campaign and White House documents, directing senior aides to testify freely, and asserting no privilege claims. And at the same time, the President took no act that in fact deprived the Special Counsel of the documents and witnesses necessary to complete his investigation."[8] Trump, however, had not consented to an interview with prosecutors, but did submit written responses to their questions.

Trump claimed "total exoneration" but Democrats in Congress were not convinced. In the Democratic controlled US House, Judiciary Committee chair Jerold Nadler (D-NY) and Intelligence Committee chair Adam Schiff (D-CA) both kept the issue alive with subsequent hearings, including anticlimactic appearances by Robert Mueller before their committees. House Speaker Nancy Pelosi (D-CA) regularly decried Trump's conduct but initially did not press for impeachment, despite growing support for it among House Democrats and Democratic partisans. African American Representative Al Green (D-TX) forced a House floor vote on his impeachment resolution, citing Trump's "bigotry and racism" on July 17, 2019. It failed 332–95 but over 40 percent of House Democrats voted for it. Trump seemed to press conflict with Democrats throughout 2019, perhaps because he believed impeachment proceedings would rebound against Democrats in the 2020 election as they had against House Republicans in 1997 when they impeached Bill Clinton. He may have been granted his wish when the House began an impeachment investigation in late September 2019.

CONCLUSION

Trump's "dominator" personality promised a highly controversial presidency, and that is what has transpired. His obsession with tweets placed him almost daily at the center of the news, but not always to his advantage. He has not employed the resources of the presidency to ensure his maximum effectiveness. High turnover of top administration positions, coupled with an initially inexperienced White House staff, got his presidency off to a rough start. Some administration officials, such as Attorney General Barr, Secretary of State Pompeo, and acting Chief of Staff Mulvaney, have brought more stability to Trump's presidency. The president's quirky and irascible personality, however, ensure that his administration will continue to be newsworthy in ways the president may not relish.

Trump's personality seeks the domination of others, seldom a recipe for success in a system of separated powers. Quiet negotiation—indeed, any form of quiet—is seldom the president's approach to his job. Trump and his White House focus daily on battles with political opponents, with little apparent consideration of the president's future power prospects.

Though Trump has secured some policy victories, as discussed in the following chapter, the ongoing staff turmoil as well as the unwillingness to fill many administrative vacancies in key agencies serve as a barrier to success. Trump himself thinks many appointments are not that essential to his administration, telling *Forbes* in October 2017: "I'm generally not going to make a lot of the appointments that would normally be—because you don't need them. I mean, you look at some of these agencies, how massive they are, and it's totally unnecessary. They have hundreds of thousands of people."[9] As a result, the administration of many programs and initiatives is placed in the hands of career employees who may not share Trump's agenda.

Trump's daily focus on colorful conflicts often displaces the quiet negotiations that can make the presidency operate effectively. The National Security Council and Defense and State departments have long functioned on the basis of quiet negotiation. The OMB, handling the president's budget proposal and legislative program, focuses on consultations with Congress often far from the media spotlight. Cabinet officers likewise go about their business without seeking the bright light of constant publicity. President Trump, with his outsized media presence and penchant for constant quarrels, often removes himself from the more constructive routines of government. There's a price to be paid for that. That price may rise with the onset of an impeachment investigation.

6

THE TRUMP AGENDA

Trump's agenda seems to vary with his daily attention span and tweets. Has he delivered on his central campaign promises? He summarized many of those in his 2015 campaign announcement speech. Trump pledged to build a wall along the border with Mexico and to deport people in the United States illegally. He promised to rejuvenate domestic manufacturing by renegotiating or abandoning trade deals, to repeal and replace the Affordable Care Act, to protect the Second Amendment, to rebuild America's infrastructure, and to protect Social Security, Medicare, and Medicaid. And, quite significantly, he pledged to reduce what he described as job-killing regulations. Trump focused much of his ire on environmental regulations which he believed to be undermining the US energy sector, especially with regard to extracting fossil fuels such as oil, natural gas, and coal.

DEREGULATION

Trump's efforts to roll back regulations have yielded greater success for the president than for most of his predecessors. Much of President Obama's domestic policy legacy, from immigration to environmental policy, was constructed using unilateral executive action and new or revised regulations issued by federal agencies under his lead. President Trump has used his power as chief executive to roll back many of those actions. In fact, as a candidate Trump promised to repeal "every single Obama executive order." Trump's promises to roll back regulations on American industry, to boost domestic energy production, and to undo Obama's environmental policy legacy could, at least in part, be accomplished via the exercise of unilateral executive authority.

On his first day in office, President Trump ordered a halt to all pending regulations to allow for review or revision. Such a move is standard practice for incoming presidents. Trump issued as well a seemingly symbolic executive order intended to "minimize the economic burden of the Affordable Care Act" also known as Obamacare. Though much of the order set the stage for future legislative action, one section directed federal agency heads to "waive, defer, grant exemptions or delay implementation of any requirements of the act that would place fiscal burdens" as a result of the Affordable Care Act. In response, the Internal Revenue Service announced that they would not implement a process for rejecting tax returns from filers who failed to indicate whether or not they had insurance coverage, undermining a central provision of the law. If younger and healthier individuals failed to comply with the mandate, and faced no tax penalty, then health insurance providers were left with older and less healthy clients who cost more to cover. This could destabilize the entire healthcare market.

In subsequent months, the administration took steps to shorten enrollment times and curtail publicity about enrollment in plans under the Affordable Care Act. The importance of Trump's regulatory and administrative actions grew when a Republican Congress in 2017 failed to pass a replacement for the Affordable Care Act, though the 2017 tax reform bill eliminated the individual mandate's tax penalty altogether.

Trump ordered a review of fuel-efficiency standards for vehicles manufactured between 2022 and 2025 that was put in place by the Obama administration. Echoing auto industry sentiment, Trump argued the new standards were too tough on the industry. The Trump administration announced plans in August 2018 to freeze fuel-efficiency requirements for the nation's cars and trucks through 2026, no small rollback. California's Attorney General immediately filed suit seeking information employed to create the rollback.

Trump also issued Executive Order 13783 in late March 2017. It directed federal agencies "review existing regulations that potentially burden the development or use of domestically produced energy resources and appropriately suspend, revise, or rescind those that unduly burden the development of domestic energy resources beyond the degree necessary to protect the public interest or otherwise comply with the law." The main target of the executive order was the Clean Power Plan, a regulation issued by the EPA under the Obama administration, which would require states to dramatically reduce carbon dioxide emissions from power plants by 32 percent below 2005 levels over the next few decades.

A coalition of Democrat-led states filed suit asking the courts to force the Trump administration to comply with the Clean Power Plan regulations, but the Trump administration responded by asking the court to delay any consideration of the legality of the Clean Power Plan until after the EPA had an opportunity to review and revise the plan. The revision arrived in August 2018. The Affordable Clean Energy Rule gave individual states more authority to make their own plans for regulating greenhouse gas emissions from coal-fired power plants. "We're ending the intrusive EPA regulations that kill jobs," Trump said in a White House statement. Litigation by opponents of the new plan immediately ensued.

Trump also lifted an Obama-imposed moratorium on coal leasing on federal lands, and ordered a review of a 2015 rule issued by the EPA, known as Waters of the United States rule, which greatly expanded the scope of federal authority over waterways in the United States. The rule placed the EPA in charge of protecting streams and wetlands from pollution and degradation—especially from the runoff produced by mining. Coupled with the Clean Power Plan, Trump said these policies represented a "war on coal." A federal district judge in April 2019 ruled the coal leasing policy violated current law and the administration contemplated an appeal.

Collectively, the policies targeted by Trump were core components of the Obama administration's Climate Action Plan (CAP) announced in 2013. The CAP was established to help the United States meet the goal, set by Obama in 2009, of reducing US greenhouse gas emissions by roughly 17 percent below 2005 levels by 2020. Critics of the CAP argued that the economic costs of the plan far outweighed the benefits, with some suggesting particularly devastating impacts on the coal industry.

With the stage set for the dismantling of the CAP, Trump announced the next step in June 2017 when he announced that the United States would withdraw from the Paris Climate Agreement. Completed in 2015, the Paris Agreement was signed by 195 nations and was intended to represent a global commitment to combat climate change, especially rising temperatures, by reducing emissions of greenhouse gasses. Under Obama, the United States agreed to reduce its greenhouse gas emissions by 26 to 28 percent below 2005 levels by 2025 and to commit up to $3 billion in aid for poorer countries by 2020. In withdrawing from the agreement, Trump made good on a frequent campaign promise to do so. Trump was able to withdraw the United States from the Paris Agreement because it was a nonbinding executive agreement signed by President Obama.

As a candidate, Donald Trump committed himself to a domestic policy agenda of reduced regulatory burdens and the promotion of greater domestic energy production. Trump's decision to dismantle the CAP and withdraw from the Paris Agreement, coupled with two presidential memoranda to revive the Dakota and Keystone XL pipelines, both halted by President Obama, represented an attempt to deliver on that commitment. President Trump was able to take these actions swiftly for a very simple reason—much of President Obama's environmental and energy policy legacy was built on unilateral executive actions—actions that a subsequent president could undo. A clear lesson of the Trump presidency is that programs created by the stroke of a pen can often be undone by the stroke of a pen.

But these pen wielding victories have been confined mostly to Trump policies and actions that are best categorized as unilateral and reactive. Trump has made effective use of the powers afforded the presidency to dismantle policies that Obama created using those same executive powers. But the fights are not over. Dozens of deregulatory actions have been litigated in federal courts and many have been overturned.

Trump also has enjoyed success in Congress as well with actions that require Congressional action to reverse executive actions. His use of the Congressional GOP of the Congressional Review Act to rescind regulations issued during the final months of the Obama administration was unprecedented. The wording of the Congressional Review Act makes it difficult for substantively similar regulations to be re-issued under a future president. But the number of pending and nonfinal regulations subject to such unilateral action is limited. There are no longer any regulations issued by Obama that are susceptible to the Congressional Review Act.

IMMIGRATION

The Trump administration's immigration initiatives did not start well. Trump's term began with a controversial ban on immigration from seven Middle Eastern counties that quickly was overruled by federal courts and withdrawn. This was an executive order that would have the status of law unless rescinded by a later president or voided by federal courts. The ban had not been vetted by the Department of Homeland Security or Department of Defense but had been the quick work of White House aides Steve Bannon and Steven Miller. It was eventually withdrawn and a revised order promulgated, again voided by the courts and then headed to the Supreme Court for final resolution. The Supreme Court preliminarily reinstated the travel ban in June 2017 but required broader exemptions from the ban for relatives of individuals living in the United States.

The administration faced immigration controversies on many fronts. In addition to its initial limits on immigration from six Muslim countries, later in 2017 it capped the number of international refugees at forty-five thousand. The administration also hoped to change federal immigration laws from a "family based" to a "merit based" system.

Then there was the controversy over the Deferred Action on Childhood Arrivals (DACA) program, which delayed deportation of those arriving as undocumented immigrants as children. The administration in September 2017 ordered termination of the program and urged Congress to pass a revised form of the program. In November, a federal judge ordered continuation of the DACA. The controversy arrived at the Supreme Court in 2019.

Trump's work with the 2017–2018 GOP Congress yielded little on immigration. Immigration reform would have to pass on a totally partisan vote because Democrats opposed administration plans. Yet the modest GOP majorities in each chamber could not reach consensus on any immigration reform plans.

Trump famously had called for a big wall on the Mexican border. Upon taking office, he directed the Department of Homeland Security to begin diverting funds for a border wall. Trump's initial budget in March 2017 called for $2.6 billion in wall funding, but Congress was slow to grant funds. This led to a Trump-instigated partial government shutdown from December 22, 2017, to January 25, 2018—the longest in US history—over his demand for $5 billion for the wall. Congress with its new Democratic majority in the House eventually agreed to give Trump $1.6 billion for the border wall and it placed some restrictions on the wall's characteristics. Shortly afterward, Trump declared a national emergency regarding the southern border and reallocated some federal spending, moving almost $8 billion toward wall construction. A federal judge blocked the reallocation but the Supreme Court in July 2019 allowed the president to spend $2.5 billion in reprogrammed Pentagon funds on the wall. In early 2019, he asked Congress for an additional $8.6 billion for the wall. In sum, Trump has made limited progress on a wall. But it is less than he promised and Mexico is not paying for it, as he claimed it would on the stump in 2016.

Meanwhile a surge of migrants crossing the Texas border in 2019 led to controversy over the conditions of their detention centers. Democrats condemned the centers as inhumane while Trump asserted that the border crisis he had proclaimed had worsened.

THE FISCAL TRUMP

Trump's promised tax cut during the 2016 campaign was fulfilled by a significant tax reduction with the help of a GOP Congress in 2017. Yet it's hard to find policy areas where Trump's promises are more distant from his actual performance than those about federal budget deficits and the national debt. During the campaign, Trump indicated that whipping the federal budget into shape would not be difficult. He told Fox News' Sean Hannity that budget balance could be accomplished "fairly quickly." He informed the *Washington Post* that he could eliminate the mammoth $19 trillion national debt over a period of eight years.

Budget trends instead got much worse under Trump. Federal budget deficits rose from $565 billion in fiscal year 2016 to an estimated $1,091 billion for fiscal year 2019 thanks to tax cuts, increased defense spending, and lax fiscal discipline in other areas of federal spending. The national debt is not shrinking but has grown by an enormous two trillion dollars under Trump. Big drivers of spending are Social Security and Medicare, each with growing funding problems. Current estimates put Medicare's insolvency date at 2026 and Social Security's at 2034. Does Trump care? Trump has pledged no major cuts or tax increases for these programs.

The main fiscal initiative under Trump has been his large tax cut, passed by the GOP Congress in 2017. It reduced five of seven personal income tax rates, raised the standard deduction from $12,000 for single people to $24,000 annually for married couples filing jointly. It capped the state and local tax and mortgage interest deductions and reduced the corporate tax rate to 21 percent, among other provisions. Many analysts believe it stimulated short-term economic growth to a vigorous 2.9 percent in 2018 and a 3.1 percent annualized rate by 2019's first quarter. The long-term impact on the federal budget and debt is much less rosy. The Congressional Budget Office did estimate that the cuts would boost the economic growth by 0.7 percent a year for ten years but would also swell the national debt by an additional $1.9 trillion dollars over that decade. When presented with the long-term budget trends by his senior officials in 2017, Trump shrugged them off with "Yeah, but I won't be here."

As Trump negotiated a bipartisan budget agreement in 2019, Senate Majority Leader Mitch McConnell (R-KY) reportedly told him that no politician has ever lost an election for spending more money. The final deal agreed to by Trump and Democratic Congressional leaders and passed by Congress reflected that sentiment. The two-year deal increased defense and domestic spending by $320 billion and suspended both the federal debt ceiling and specific statutory spending caps. Any tough choices would have to come after the 2020 elections. Meanwhile, deficits would amount to about $1 trillion (that's a thousand billion) annually and the national debt would continue to mushroom.

JUDGES, JUDGES, JUDGES

Few candidates have made more specific promises about federal judicial appointments. Trump has pretty much followed through on these promises. He took the unprecedented step early in the 2016 campaign of releasing a list of eleven candidates he would consider as replacements for the deceased Supreme Court Justice Antonin J. Scalia. In addition to this May 2016 list of eleven possible nominees, he added another ten names in September. On this second list was Neil Gorsuch, a consistent judicial conservative who became Trump's first nominee, confirmed by a largely party line 54–46 vote by the Senate on April 7, 2017.

The retirement of Anthony Kennedy, the vital swing vote on the court, in late June 2018 led to a firestorm of controversy surrounding Trump's nomination of Brett Kavanaugh, a former law clerk for Kennedy and then judge on the important US Court of Appeals of the District of Columbia Circuit. Kavanaugh's nomination promised to solidify a 5–4 conservative majority on the court. A number of women charged Kavanaugh with sexual harassment, most notably Christine Blasey Ford, a California college professor. Her passionate testimony before the Senate Judiciary Committee was followed by Kavanaugh's rebuttal of her allegations before the committee. Kavanaugh ultimately won confirmation because corroborating evidence for this accuser's allegations failed to surface. Trump has promised to nominate additional conservatives to the court if future vacancies arise.

The Trump administration also placed high priority on nominating and confirming conservatives to federal district courts and circuit courts of appeals. Don McGann, the initial White House Counsel, spearheaded the confirmation effort with the enthusiastic cooperation of Senate Majority Leader Mitch McConnell (R-KY). By August 2019, Trump had secured 145 successful confirmations, compared with Obama's 95 and George W. Bush's 145 at comparable points in their first terms. Trump's big success, however, came at the level of the circuit courts of appeals, which often issue consequential decisions about federal and constitutional questions. Trump's forty-three successful circuit court nominees allowed him to flip a majority of these courts to majorities of GOP-appointed judges. His forty-three new circuit judges also dwarfed Obama's nineteen and George W. Bush's twenty-six at comparable points in their terms. This record helped to endear Trump to conservatives, whatever his possible transgressions from their ideological orthodoxy on other issues.

Despite his judicial confirmation successes, Trump otherwise has struggled in his relations with Congress, now made worse with a Democratic House and government shutdown. Immigration reform, new international trade agreements, the annual budget and modernizing America's aging infrastructure all occupy a spot on Trump's agenda and none can be accomplished without Congress. Progress on these fronts during the remainder of his first term seems a long shot. Many federal agencies still suffer from staff vacancies which limit their ability to revise and review existing policies, let alone develop and issue new ones.

TRUMP'S FOREIGN POLICY

During his run for the presidency, Donald Trump stated a variety of shifting positions about foreign policy challenges facing the nation. But one thing never changed: his encompassing campaign slogans of "America First" and "Make America Great Again." For him, America was always "losing" by engaging in unfair trade deals, failing to restrict illegal immigration, and acting as the world's policeman while other nations failed to adequately fund their own defense.

What did "America First" and "Make America Great Again" connote during the 2016 campaign? His approach started with a harsh critique of foreign policy in recent decades, particularly under Barack Obama.

In contrast, Trump promised to significantly boost military spending, demand allies pay more for their defense, demonstrate more consistent support for allies (including Israel and eastern European nations), adopt more aggressive policies toward China and North Korea, and create a more coherent foreign policy based on "American interests and the shared interests of our allies."[1]

INTERNATIONAL TRADE

Once in office, trade policy became a showcase for Trump's aggressive nationalism. Trump criticized Germany and China for their huge balance of trade surpluses with the United States while also pledging to renegotiate the North America Free Trade Agreement to get better terms from Canada and Mexico. That negotiation led to a new agreement among the three nations announced in 2018 with Congressional approval still pending.

The administration's initial approach to international trade started with a withdrawal from the Trans-Pacific Partnership negotiations and agreement. The agreement negotiated by the Obama administration sought to reduce trade barriers among the United States and eleven Asian nations. One goal of the agreement was to enhance trade with Asian nations other than with China, which was not included in the pact. Trump instead intended to deal with China trade problems on a bilateral basis.

That led to lengthy negotiations with China over several nagging trade issues. First, Trump decried large annual trade deficits with

China—$539.5 billion in 2018—though many economists dismissed the concern as unimportant to the nation's economic health. Second, China restricts market access by US firms to joint ventures with Chinese companies which promotes technology transfer to Chinese interests. Third, China's thorough disclosure rules for new product sales in China can facilitate theft of US technology. Fourth, China may encourage currency manipulation to flood foreign markets with cheap goods. Fifth, government subsidies also can make Chinese products unfairly cheap in the US domestic market.[2]

From 2017 to 2019, the two nations gradually increased the amount of retaliatory tariffs aimed at each other but also negotiated to address trade issues. By early 2018, the administration thought it was close to a deal with Chinese negotiators on a number of these issues but certain Chinese concessions were then abruptly withdrawn. Trump in May claimed China "broke the deal" and threatened punishing tariffs against the Chinese. The administration announced tariffs on $200 billion in Chinese goods and began planning to raise tariffs to as high as $540 billion in Chinese products; China responded by promising its own tariffs on $60 billion of US goods. The tariffs promised short-term pain for both economies in the form of higher prices and slower economic growth. The two nations imposed additional trade barriers in 2019 as negotiations faltered. Trump committed to an important policy and political gamble as his reelection campaign approach.

The Trump administration acted because of their view that China was seeking long-term control over vital international technology, an outcome inimical to American economic and security interests. Further, America's economic health in 2019 made this a good time to act before Chinese supremacy became unstoppable. So the Trump administration was willing to take a short-term political risk in order to prevent what it saw as dangerous Chinese attempts to gain superiority over the US economy.[3]

Trump in June 2019 engaged in a trade gamble with Mexico. The large influx of asylum seekers across the southern border, likely to total over one million in 2019, led Trump to threaten to impose escalating tariffs on all imported Mexican goods. The tariffs would begin at five percent and escalate to 25 percent if Mexico and the United States did not reach an agreement on enhanced border security. Trump took this action against the advice of his trade negotiator and senior White House staff. Mexico then agreed to send several thousand national guard troops to secure the border with the United States and to hold migrants while they sought adjudication of their asylum claims. Trump claimed a victory for border security and his aggressive trade tactics. Time would tell if the agreement actually stemmed the tide of illegal immigration across the border with Mexico.

NORTH KOREA

As he left the presidency, Barack Obama informed Donald Trump that the most urgent problem he would face was North Korea's attempts to build intercontinental ballistic missiles. Signs soon appeared after inauguration day that North Korea was planning more missile tests. Trump's options were limited. The United States could continue an intensified cyber and electronic warfare begun under Obama, attempt to reopen negotiations that had yielded little in the past, prepare for missile strikes on launch facilities that promised uncertain results, or encourage China to more aggressively pressure North Korea to desist.

A tit-for-tat with North Korea transpired in 2017. North Korea fired four ballistic test missiles into the Sea of Japan on March 2. This led to the United States dispatching missile defense ships to the area later in the month. Evidence mounted of continued nuclear weapons tests by North Korea, and two unsuccessful ballistic missile launches occurred in March and April. The rogue nation was conducting missile and nuclear tests at its most rapid pace ever. The North Korean issue again arose at the United Nations Security Council on April 19. Russia vetoed a resolution condemning the most recent nuclear test as in violation of international arms control accords.

Trump then tried a diplomatic overture on May 1, indicating he would be "honored" to meet with Kim Jong Un in direct one-to-one talks. North Korea responded with three ballistic missile launches in May and one in early June. Its first successful tests of intercontinental ballistic missiles came in July, raising a new security threat to America itself. In early August, the UN Security Council unanimously passed new sanctions targeting North Korea's primary exports, with even Russia voting in favor this time. Once North Korea threatened to strike Guam with its missiles, the president harshly countered with a guarantee of "fire and fury" if such aggression occurred.[4] Administration officials meanwhile offered assurances that war with the rogue regime was not imminent.

Trump then tried the diplomatic route, meeting twice with Kim Jong Un, in Singapore on June 12, 2017, and in Hanoi on February 27–28, 2018. By the end of the second summit, Trump's demands that North Korea denuclearize had not been met. He attempted to restart negotiations in June 2019 by staging a brief step into North Korea to shake hands with Kim. North Korea nevertheless continued its missile tests. The options available to Trump when he took office had not changed. The administration pursued increasing cooperation and engagement with China, Japan and South Korea over the issue, along with development of antimissile capability and cyberwarfare activities against Kim Jong Un's regime. That approach bought time but did not remove the underlying problem—the expansionist aggressiveness of North Korea.

THE MIDDLE EAST

The Syrian civil war presented President Trump with a complex set of problems that obstructed development of a clear and constructive way forward for the United States. First, the myriad factions in the conflict—Assad and his Russian and Iranian sponsors, a collection of anti-Assad rebels including the Kurdish ethnic group and the ISIS "caliphate" occupying considerable Syrian territory—made sorting through them a big challenge, as Obama had found in previous years. Obama's embrace of a nuclear deal with Iran made him unwilling to risk direct engagement with the pro-Iranian groups supporting President Assad. Trump had no such qualms, evident in his authorizing in early April 2017 a strike of fifty-nine tomahawk missiles on a pro-Assad military base in response to reports of the regime's use of chemical weapons on unarmed civilians. This humanitarian response received widespread praise.

By December 2018, however, Trump had had enough of the Syria mission and publicly vowed to remove all of the remaining two thousand US troops from there, claiming ISIS had been defeated. This prompted the resignation of Defense Secretary James Mattis, which Trump accelerated by moving up Mattis's planned resignation date. Never mind. By the beginning of March he had reassured Senate Republicans that the troops would remain in Syria to ensure ISIS did not revive there, and they did.

After initially tolerating Obama's diplomatic agreement with Iran, Trump did withdraw from the agreement in May 2018. Acknowledging Iran had abided by the letter of the agreement, he argued that the agreement itself did nothing to curtail Iran's sponsorship of regional terrorism and pursuit of nuclear weapons. He also announced extensive economic sanctions on the regime. Trump's secretary of state, Mike Pompeo, supported the move, in contrast to his predecessor Rex Tillerson. European signatories remained committed to the agreement. Iran lashed out with denunciations of the United States. Over the next year, the sanctions hit hard because America's trading partners did not want to risk their US markets by trading with Iran. On the one-year anniversary of Trump's announced withdrawal from the agreement, the administration placed additional sanctions on Iran. The administration continued to label Iran as a leading "state sponsor of terrorism" in Syria and throughout the Middle East as Trump's harsh sanctions hit the nation. Iran responded by restarting parts of its nuclear development program by capturing British tankers in the vital Strait of Hormuz. Intelligence sources indicated that Iran was the nation that launched a devastating drone attack on a Saudi oil refinery in September 2019.

Trump's initial tendency to delegate to his generals was evident in the administration's Afghanistan policy. In June Secretary of Defense Mattis announced the additional deployment of a few thousand troops to the nation and promised an overall strategy by midsummer. Despite Trump's misgivings, Trump approved a continued deployment. By that point, the stalemate between the Afghan government and its Taliban-ISIS foes had been long-standing. In subsequent months, Trump frequently lamented the continued US presence in Afghanistan and publicly considered withdrawal. The hawkish Trump advisors who succeeded the generals—Secretary of State Pompeo and National Security Advisor John Bolton—remained firmly committed to military involvement in the country. The long-term deployment seemed likely to continue under Trump, along with its steady stream of US casualties.

Trump long had voiced support for Israel and demonstrated his closeness and support for Prime Minister Binyamin Netanyahu. Trump officially recognized Jerusalem as the capital of Israel on December 6, 2017, a move warmly welcomed by Netanyahu. Attempts to create a negotiated peace between Israel and the Palestinian Authority produced little progress in the announcement's wake. Trump also favored Sunni Arab nations who were outspoken rivals of Iran. The president underscored his interest in improved relations with the Sunni Islamic government during a visit to Saudi Arabia in late May. Visiting Saudi Arabia in May 2017, he met with Egyptian President al-Sisi and Saudi King Salman. He was warmly received by the Saudi government which had difficult relations with the Obama administration and strongly objected to Obama's Iranian nuclear accord.

EUROPE AND RUSSIA

"America First" to Trump does not involve the same sort of close diplomatic alignment with Europe that had characterized the Obama administration. Trump also has criticized the open immigration policies of

Germany, Sweden, and other European nations, while touting the tighter immigration restrictions of eastern European nations like Hungary. Trump's approach to Europe suggests a more unilateral and much less multilateral orientation toward international relations. That unpredictability, he believes, is an asset for the United States internationally in that it keeps opponents guessing. It also makes Europe quite nervous about differences with his administration over common defense, climate change, immigration, and trade. That's no small list.

When the Obama administration agreed to the Paris Climate Accord on October 5, 2016, Trump issued a statement labeling it a "bad deal" that would "impose enormous costs on American households through higher electricity prices and higher taxes." All European governments had signed the accord. Trump officially withdrew the United States from the accord on June 2, 2017. In the wake of his withdrawal, many state and local governments agreed to voluntary alliances to try to fulfill the goals of the Paris accord.

Trump in office backtracked on his hostility to NATO during the 2016 campaign. Though he declared it "obsolete" on the eve of his inauguration on January 17, by April 12 he admitted that he made his January comment "not knowing much about NATO" and assuming it did little to fight terrorism. He had since learned otherwise: "They made a change and now they do fight terrorism. I said it was obsolete. It is no longer obsolete."

How has policy toward Russia shifted in the Trump presidency? The administration coordinated a more aggressive military response to ISIS with Russia. Yet the White House has also directed bombing against Syrian President Assad, a Russian client, in response to evidence of humanitarian atrocities by Assad's regime. The Congress overwhelmingly passed enhanced sanctions on Russia, which the White House did sign. In short, no major redirection in Russian policy has yet appeared despite the president's repeated statements of willingness to work with Putin on issues of mutual interest.

Trump did, however, institute partial policy change toward the former Russian client state of Cuba. Trump kept the US embassy open but placed new travel and commercial restrictions on Cuba in 2018 and 2019. He prohibited commerce with companies owned by Cuban intelligence services and the military and more strictly enforced the granting of travel exemptions to the island, making it much harder for US citizens to visit the island.

CONCLUSION

Donald Trump's time in the presidency has produced much sound and fury and a flurry of executive orders and memoranda altering previous policies. In those ways he has shaken up Washington. His direction of foreign policy has been controversial. Trump embraces the "permanent campaign" in office, trafficking in and relishing conflict in his public statements and personal tweets. His inexperience with diplomatic negotiations has brought him trouble. His controversial phone call with Ukrainian president Zelensky launched impeachment investigations by House Democrats.

Despite all the noise, Trump has had some policy successes. His 2017 tax cut seems to have stimulated short-term economic growth. He managed to get a bipartisan criminal justice reform bill passed in 2018. The success of many of his domestic and foreign policies, however, remain in the "to be determined" category. His aggressive trade policies may inflict economic costs on Americans and may or may not succeed in getting better trade arrangements. His hard line against Iran could produce armed conflict or a Middle East friendlier to US interests. His battles with the Democratic House may derail any hope of additional bipartisan legislation in the wake of impeachment proceedings. The possible outcomes will have big impacts on the 2020 presidential election, the subject of our final chapter.

Here's a scorecard on his promises so far. He has indeed "shaken up" Washington with his conflictual style, frequent turnover of appointees, and large number of positions left unfilled. Trump daily fulfills his promise to call out the "fake news" he perceives issuing from the establishment media. He has made some progress on a border wall, but far less than was promised. Broader immigration reform is stalled. As promised, he has cut taxes and regulations, but has fallen far short regarding his campaign assurances about cutting spending, deficits, and the national debt. He has followed through by successfully appointing conservative federal judges in considerable numbers. In foreign policy, where presidents have great sway, he has implemented an "America First" foreign policy that is nationalist, aggressive on trade, and challenging to the international order. Yet his reckless language during a diplomatic phone call has brought him to the verge of impeachment by a Democratically controlled US House.

Does all this position him well for reelection?

7

TRUMP'S FUTURE

Trump's pugnacious statements and tweets, showcasing his penchant for unproductive verbal conflict, are part of the reason why America's politics now feature bitter political division. His ongoing verbal fusillade has helped to bring him to the verge of impeachment. But the reasons for national division and contentiousness extend far beyond Trump himself. Over the last thirty years, US politics have grown increasingly more polarized between Democrats and Republicans. Two aspects characterize the polarization. First, those who are politically active divide strongly on many major issues before the country. Second, within the two parties their activists hold relatively uniform issue positions. Trump's querulous persona just adds fuel to this fire.

To the picture of Trump and polarization we must add three traits of the current political situation that will determine Trump's future prospects as president. First, economic conditions, particularly rising inequality and the loss of US manufacturing jobs to foreign competitors, helped to shape a growing popular discontent with politics as usual. The discontent encompasses low trust that government will do "what is right" and a widespread belief that it cares little for the concerns of ordinary citizens.[1] A result is a political era of "partisan volatility" in which governing alignments are unstable. Trump's rise is both symptom and product of that volatility. That volatility is also a major impediment to his future governing and electoral success.

DEFINING TRAITS OF CONTEMPORARY US POLITICS

Rising economic inequality and the loss of many high-quality US manufacturing jobs have roiled US politics in recent decades and helped propel Donald Trump into the White House. The US Census Bureau has charted a steady rise in income inequality since 1993.

By 2014, "the top 5% of households received 21.8% of 'equivalence-adjusted' aggregate income, while the bottom 60% received just 27.1%. Equivalence-adjusted estimates factor in different household sizes and compositions."[2] Despite a 5.2 percent increase in middle-class incomes in 2015, income inequality remained stable.[3] Wealth differences have grown even more pronounced. A Pew Center report found that in 2013, the median net worth of the nation's upper-income families was 6.6 times that of middle-income families, and nearly 70 times that of lower-income families. The analysis also found that since 1983, virtually all the wealth gains made by US families have gone to the upper-income group.[4]

Lots of Americans feel they are economically falling behind as time passes. The nation's middle class has suffered from income stagnation and rising personal debt in recent decades. Aggregate incomes in 2015 remained 1.6 percent lower than in 2000 and 2.4 percent below the 1999 peak. Median earnings for men working full time remained lower than they were in the 1970s.[5] The Federal Reserve reported in 2013 that the average debt of middle-class families—those that fall within the middle three-fifths of the population by earnings—amounted to an estimated 122 percent of annual income, nearly double the level of 1989.[6]

The stagnation of male income reflects the big loss of US manufacturing since its peak in 1979. The Bureau of Labor Statistics reported that by 2015, 7,231,000 such jobs had disappeared since 1979, a 37 percent decline.[7] The rise of automation and strong foreign competition spawned this decline.

Edward Alden, Senior Fellow at the Council of Foreign Relations, summarizes the import of all these statistical trends. "The United States has faced increased import competition in a growing number of economic sectors that once employed millions of people at generally higher wages than they could earn at other jobs. . . . Those who lose their jobs to computers are likely to find news ones, while those who lose their jobs to imports are much less likely to do so." The implications for many middle-class Americans are ominous: "But far too many Americans are simply unprepared for the competition they are now in. They are like overmatched boxers who keep getting knocked down, only to be told by their corner that they just have to get back in the ring and keep taking the punches in the hope that eventually they will become better fighters."[8] It is precisely this discontent that candidate Trump exploited with his assaults on foreign trade and assertion that "America doesn't win anymore."

Americans' political attitudes shifted as these economic trends persisted. Alongside Americans' income and debt difficulties came widespread and growing popular discontent with government, a trend that began in the late 1960s and persisted through the 2016 election. The immediate causes of the discontent were divisive events of the sixties and seventies: Vietnam, the civil rights revolution, and Watergate, along with the persistent economic problems of the 1970s.

As we noted in our first chapter, University of Michigan surveys since 1960 have asked four questions about trust in government—a "trust index" and also a question about popular discontent, querying whether government officials "care much about what people like me think." The measures vary inversely—lower trust and higher discontent—in a strong pattern since 1964.[9] By 2016, trust in government remained quite low and popular discontent quite high. The political outsider Donald Trump, with no governmental experience but great personal wealth and a vivid media profile, could echo these views effectively—and did. His "drain the swamp" mantra was effective political shorthand that both diagnosed the problem and pointed toward a solution.

In the short term at least, the economy has prospered under Trump despite his ongoing trade war with China. Economic growth under Trump rose from 2.2 percent in 2017 to a healthy 2.9 percent in 2018. Unemployment among the overall workforce had dropped to 3.7 percent by July 2019, down from 5 percent two years before. Black and Latino unemployment in July 2019 stood at 6.0 percent and 4.5 percent respectively, both near record lows. Yet Trump remains unpopular with job approval mired in the low forties and faces a tough reelection battle. Some of this popular disfavor results from Trump's own controversial behavior and the heated denunciations of his opponents. But the roots of his problems also lie in the broader political era.

Trump took office during what political scientist Byron Shafer astutely calls an "era of political volatility," begun during Bill Clinton's presidency, featuring a wide range of electoral outcomes, a "kaleidoscope" of "limitless electoral possibilities in very short order."[10] Trump is the latest electoral surprise in this sequence, following the partisan zig zag of the Clinton, George W. Bush, and Obama presidencies, featuring Republican, Democratic, and divided partisan Congresses.

For Shafer, our era of political volatility has several major features. The first is a close national partisan balance between the two major parties. The rise of Republican dominance in the conservative but previously Democratic south and of Democratic dominance in the more liberal and previously electorally competitive northeast helped to produce a growing ideological polarization across issue domains that are aligned, resulting in a nationalization of American party politics. The second trait of ideological polarization between the parties received reinforcement via the rising dominance of ideological thinking among party activists and even elected officials, making polarization widespread across geographical regions and levels of government.

Ideological politics produced a third trait, in which all issue conflicts gradually lined up along the partisan, ideological divide: "All the great policy domains of the modern world—economic welfare, foreign affairs, civil rights, and cultural values—collapsed into one dimension, liberals versus conservatives by way of Democrats versus Republicans." When all issues are fought on one partisan front, governmental stagnation will frequently occur when partisan control of government is divided between the parties, as it was from 1995–2001, 2007–2009, 2013–2017, and since the 2018 midterm elections that gave Democrats control of the US House.

National policymaking is "characterized by long stretches of intense partisan warfare, interrupted only intermittently by spikes of legislative activity, the product of which was often omnibus legislation, bundling a set of major concerns that could relieve the pressure for action while allocating rewards on all sides." Major partisan legislative breakthroughs included Bill Clinton's economic stimulus bill of 1993, George W. Bush's tax cuts of 2001, and Barack Obama's economic stimulus in 2009 and Affordable Care Act in 2010. Examples of bipartisan omnibus legislative breakthroughs included a budget deal in 1995, a tax cut in 2011, and fiscal legislation to reopen the government in 2013.

Into this environment walked President Donald Trump. Before we undertake a detailed inventory of his prospects, it's worth noting some immediate consequences for Trump from the three characteristics of his "political time" that we have just sketched.

Wage stagnation and trade and automation-based job losses were highlighted by candidate Trump, so improvement on those fronts is essential to his successful presidency. Indeed, some short-term improvement has already occurred. Though Trump, the outsider candidate, capitalized on distrust of government and popular discontent during the 2016 campaign, these features of public opinion have—unhelpfully for Trump—persisted. A "kaleidoscopic" national political order, where anything is possible, threatens to disrupt his presidency. Things can go well or poorly in very short order, as the sudden onset of impeachment politics indicates. Trump is not the beneficiary of a durable electoral coalition or a dominant political party. So far, his public standing has proven problematic for his future prospects.

DONALD TRUMP'S POLITICAL CAPITAL

To figure out Trump's prospects, it's necessary to introduce the term "political capital." The concept involves several important indicators of presidential governance and public support: presidential job approval, support for the president's party, and Congressional support for the president. An additional measure involves the number of executive branch appointments available to the president. A better indicator of "appointment capital" for Trump in his early presidency is how many appointments he has made and have been confirmed by the Senate. The president's early appointment record reveals how well he is using this capital asset at the outset of his administration.

A president with high political capital will enjoy job approval from popular majorities, head a political party enjoying more favorable opinion from the public than its major party rival and receive high levels of success with his legislation on the House and Senate floors. In addition, high political capital is evident in a large number of successful executive branch appointments early in a president's administration. How does Trump stack up in these regards?

Useful indexes of public approval of a president's job performance, updated daily, appear on statistical guru Nate Silver's website *FiveThirtyEight*. There, almost all publicly released polls of presidential job approval are folded into an index of job approval. Website analysts weigh a poll's contribution to the index based on the poll's "methodological standards" and historical accuracy. Three daily approval/disapproval averages appear of all polls, polls of likely and registered voters and polls of all adults.

Trump's public approval trends since his inauguration are exceptional. No president since presidential approval surveys began in the middle 1930s has had such low approval and high disapproval in the first eight months in office. On inauguration day, Trump's approval average for all polls was 45.5 percent, for surveys of all adults 45 percent and for polls of likely and registered voters only 41 percent. This proved to be Trump's "high water mark" in polling thus far in his first term. By March 17, 2019, popular majorities in all surveys and surveys of adults disapproved of his job performance and two days later majorities in polls of registered and likely voters expressed disapproval. Since then, Trump's job approval has been "majority negative" on all three poll indexes, with his job approval hovering in the low to mid-forties. It's unlikely to improve during the nation's impeachment drama.

Trump's unprecedented early unpopularity stemmed from his stunning election victory despite losing the popular vote and his combative behavior both as candidate and president. No president upon winning election has faced such vociferous "resistance" by hostile interests and elected officials. The "resisters" employed an extraordinary range of oppositional tactics. Efforts were undertaken to encourage presidential electors to switch their votes away from Trump, force recounts in closely contested states, boycott the inauguration, block or delay presidential appointments, leak unflattering information about Trump, sue to remove the president under the emoluments clause of the Constitution, declare Trump unfit for office under the Twenty-Fifth Amendment, judicially block executive orders, and promise impending impeachment.

The intensity fueling such tactics was reflected in many recent surveys indicating that those who "strongly disapprove" of the job performance by the president consistently stand at over 40 percent and almost double the percentage "strongly approving" of the president. In polling, Trump's political capital stands at an unprecedented low. The main reasons mentioned by poll respondents for disapproving of the president are his character and personality. It may be difficult for the president to overcome widespread dislike for him as a person. The president himself reportedly accepts that he will never be broadly popular and thus concentrates his policies and communications on his "base" of 2016 supporters. Does that win him reelection?

Trump's election did not produce a popular surge in favorable views of the Republican Party. The nonpartisan Pew Center has found that favorable views of the GOP have lagged behind those of Democrats since

2010, with GOP favorable averaging just below 40 percent during that time.[11] In January 2019 Gallup found 37 percent of adults had a favorable view of the Republicans while 45 percent had positive views of the Democratic Party.[12] The GOP also has fewer identifiers than Democrats, a long-term trend still evident in 2019. National polls found Republican identification often under 30 percent, trailing Democrats by a few points. The big GOP losses in the 2018 US House elections reflected the Republican Party's unpopularity as well. Republicans lost forty House seats, control of the chamber, and garnered only 45.2 percent of the nationwide House vote compared to the Democrats' 53.1 percent.

During the GOP Congress of 2017 and 2018, Trump did score very high Congressional support in floor votes on which his administration had taken a position. His 98.7 percent success rate in 2017 was the highest recorded since tabulation began in 1954 and in 2018 it was almost as high at 93.4 percent.[13] Even so, the administration failed to move legislation on some important priorities. Repealing and replacing Obama's Affordable Care Act passed the House by only a two-vote margin in 2017 and then stalled in the Senate. Annual budget negotiations remained difficult even with his party controlling Congress because Trump, unlike many GOP legislators, has no interest in limiting entitlement spending. Trump's plans for big infrastructure projects and immigration reform have failed to produce legislative progress. The arrival of a vociferously anti-Trump Democratic House in 2019 shrank his success in Congress considerably.

Trump's presidential success ultimately derives from his levels of political capital. As we wrote in an earlier book: "The decline in political capital has produced great difficulties for presidential leadership in recent decades. It is difficult to claim warrants for leadership in an era when job approval, Congressional support and partisan affiliation provide less backing for a president than in times past. Because of the uncertainties of political capital, recent presidents has adopted a governing style that is personalized, preemptive and, at times, isolated."[14]

Trump's style indeed is personalized, preemptive, and at times isolated. He continues to showcase the outsized media persona that characterized his business career and his presidential campaign. Trump's tweets certainly are highly personal. A "preemptive" president "is not out to establish, uphold or salvage any political orthodoxy. Theirs is an unabashedly mongrel politics; it is an aggressive critique of the prevailing political categories."[15] Preemptive presidents included Richard Nixon, Woodrow Wilson, and Bill Clinton, each trying to chart his own way without careful observance of previous political orthodoxies. Nixon proved less conservative than previous GOP presidents, Clinton more centrist, and Wilson more progressive than previous Democrats. Each encountered serious political challenges—impeachment charges brought against Clinton, invalidism born of political defeat for Wilson, and probable impeachment and subsequent resignation for Nixon. Trump also encounters widespread calls for his impeachment.

Trump's political career is one of a preemptive outsider. His policies on infrastructure, foreign policy, trade, and immigration have proven divisive and controversial among US Representatives and Senators of his own party. So far, however, he enjoys very high support among Republicans in public opinion polls. Rival Democrats very much recoil from his idiosyncratic political approach. He clearly seeks to rearrange preexisting political categories by creating a new GOP coalition featuring increased numbers of white working-class voters. Preemptive presidents tend to arouse opposition from those attached to previous political ideologies and alignments. It is a dangerous presidential path.

One clear and present danger for the president is a difficult media environment, one he helped to create and now cannot escape. The president early in his term expressed surprise at the strongly negative media coverage he continues to receive. He remains the target of anonymous leaks, some of them of dubious accuracy, seized upon by reporters. Many in the bureaucracies and organizations of "permanent Washington" plant such stories in order to impede Trump's presidency. The anonymous "whistleblower" report leading to the impeachment battle is a particularly striking example of this.

Trump invited such treatment with his fiery condemnation of conventional Washington politics both as a candidate and in office. His controversial and at times peculiar and inaccurate tweets do little to burnish his credibility with a skeptical media or with many in the public beyond his minority base of supporters. Once the media fixes on a hostile narrative—in this case the story of the uncouth and unqualified President Trump—it's difficult for any president to escape the problem. The long persistence of the "Trump-Russia collusion" story, despite no major evidence in its support, is an example of Trump's media predicament. So is the strongly negative coverage of Trump's actions that have led to an impeachment investigation.

Donald Trump's initial political capital in the White House has proven to be pretty low. Add to that Trump's flamboyant and combative presidential style, a difficult relationship with the media and the Democratic US House, and the result is an extraordinary White House denizen who is tempting political fate. The unusual politics of a preemptive president invite few reliable allies over time. Political isolation can result, portending big trouble for the president's party. That is a possibility for Trump's presidential future, one of several we next explore.

TRIUMPHANT TRUMP?

Consider this rosy scenario. Donald Trump rises from his administration's inauspicious beginnings to become a successful president and a dominant political force. A string of major policy successes along with changes in the president's behavior produces his political rebound. Legislatively, this entails passage and popularity of the American Health Care Act, the GOP replacement of Obama's Affordable Care Act. Congress also then passes tax cuts and tax reform and a large spending bill to improve the nation's infrastructure—all acceptable to and celebrated by the White House and large segments of the public. The economy jells with unemployment dropping. Trump's administration increases its pace of judicial and administrative appointments and these appointments receive quicker Congressional approval. In foreign policy, Trump's trade policies produce better deals for the United States, ISIS suffers conclusive defeat, and the threat of international terrorism abates. Iran abandons its nuclear program under the pressure of US sanctions. Trump also finds a way to contain North Korea short of regional war.

The president improves his twitter strategy, resulting in better media coverage. The avalanche of anonymous, damaging leaks abates as he enjoys policy successes. Trump's popularity with political independents grows and for the first time in his presidency he enjoys majority public approval. Republicans hold Congress in the 2018 midterms and Trump arrives at 2020 in a strong position for reelection.

Some of this has happened during Trump's tenure. The tax cut spurred economic growth and low unemployment. ISIS suffered major defeat, negotiations with North Korea have begun. Administration judicial appointments and confirmations continue at a notable pace. What has kept Trump from triumph?

Important legislative initiatives in health care, immigration, and infrastructure have stalled. Trade negotiations with China have yet to produce constructive results. Trump has not improved his public image or Twitter strategy. He remains unpopular with Democrats and those vital political independents, helping to produce a Democratic takeover of the US House in the 2018 elections and an impeachment inquiry. Despite some successes, the widespread personal unpopularity of the president keeps him well short of a triumphant first term.

If Trump somehow manages to rack up a string of Congressional and foreign policy successes, change his tweet strategy, improve his media treatment and his White House management, he might become more dominant in US politics. This seems quite a long shot, because of Trump's preemptive, seemingly unchangeable and quarrelsome political style. He remains a stranger to many GOP policymakers, an enemy to many in the media, and is anathema to practically all Democrats and a majority of political independents. His inexperience and impulsiveness in office—evident in his notorious phone conversation with the Ukrainian president—may well prevent the future successes his presidency so sorely needs with legislation and foreign affairs.

DECLINE AND FALL?

This worst-case scenario begins with impeachment investigations by several US House committees concerning Trump's behavior in office. Trump encounters strong political attacks. The House Democratic majority votes approval of several articles of impeachment, though the GOP Senate defeats impeachment articles drawn up by Democrats.

Trump then limps through the remainder of his term as a greatly damaged president, unable to effectively direct domestic or foreign policy. Though his tweets remain as tart as ever, his sympathetic audience shrinks far below his 2016 popular base. Media coverage remains overwhelmingly negative. The 2020 election proves disastrous for the GOP. Along the way, foreign policy reversals on trade, North Korea, and in the Middle East worsen Trump's political standing.

Public opinion on impeachment is potentially ominous for Trump. Surveys in 2019 indicate that at least 40 percent of US adults favor some form of impeachment proceedings against the president. Previous presidents George W. Bush and Bill Clinton also incurred pro-impeachment sentiments of over 30 percent in polls. Trump's high numbers reflect his provocative personality and the greater partisan polarization of the country. Large majorities of Democrats wanted impeachment proceedings to begin, but about half of Independents and only a minority of Republicans agree.

So "many shoes have to drop" before Trump experiences a fall from office during his first term. His preemptive presidency, volatile personality, negative media coverage, and a deeply polarized nation brimming with partisan "resistance" make this a greater possibility than any president has experienced since Bill Clinton. Yet so far, not many of the conditions for his removal from the presidency before the 2020 elections are in place.

MORE OF THE SAME?

What might produce a future trajectory for Trump similar to that of his early years in office? First, Trump's base, the focus of much of his presidential persuasion, would have to stick with him. Since all the president's sweeping campaign promises on immigration, economics, and trade are not very likely to become reality, "Trump nation" will have to demonstrate considerable patience as his term transpires. So far, according to polls, they have.

Second, Democrats would continue to oppose and obstruct the president in Congress and in elections. That is certainly a safe bet, given impeachment investigations and activities of the "resistance" since Election Day 2016. Democrats may discover, however, that simply being anti-Trump is not a winning formula.

Trump may be aided by the extremism voiced by many 2020 Democratic presidential candidates. Many leading candidates, including Senators Elizabeth Warren (MA), Bernie Sanders (VT), and Kamala Harris (CA) support sweeping changes that lack majority support in opinion polls—abolishing private medical insurance, the Immigration and Customs Enforcement Agency, and promoting de facto open borders. Such positions are teed up for Trump's 2020 exploitation. Trump also is attempting to define the party in terms of its most radical members. His tweet attacks on "the Squad" of four first-term, female racial minority and leftist members of the US House—Alexandria Ocasio-Cortez (NY), Ilhan Omar (MN), Aryanna Pressley (MA), and Rashida Tlaib (MI)—indicate that strategy.

In this scenario, anonymous leaks and continuous stories about a quirky and peculiar Trump would continue to dominate the media. Over time, however, the effect of the media coverage changes fewer minds among the public. In a polarized America, many citizens choose media sources reflecting their partisan and ideological biases. After several months, media coverage of impeachment and other controversies serves to merely reinforce existing public divisions about Trump. The "news" about Trump doesn't get better or worse in its content or political effect.

"More of the same" requires Republicans to retain control of Congress while Trump's fellow partisans in the legislature work fitfully with a mercurial and inexperienced chief executive. Two thousand nineteen's divided partisan control of Congress and impeachment disputes shift that situation further against Trump. The stability scenario does require that the 2020 presidential election be competitive. A controversial GOP candidate faces off against a decidedly liberal Democratic rival with the outcome very much in doubt. That's probable.

How does the country fare with more of the same? Impeachment ends with a GOP controlled Senate failing to convict Trump by the needed sixty-seven votes. The economy grows slowly but perhaps steadily, little progress is made containing the North Korean threat, deficits continue as the public debt grows. National healthcare policy remains replete with problems as Medicaid and Medicare costs inexorably rise. The nation's infrastructure continues to be very much in need of repair. ISIS recedes but US involvement in Middle East does not. Iran remains an unresolved problem. Environmental policy remains in reverse from the Obama years. The cultural civil war between identity politics liberals and social conservatives rages on.

Meanwhile, America remains acutely divided between liberals and conservatives, Republicans and Democrats. The divisions ensure stasis, more of the same. Popular discontent and low trust in government persist as they have since the 1960s. Donald Trump, the incendiary president, frequently fuels the conflicts but maintains a cantankerous course that fails to alter the prospects for his presidency or the nation.

FOUR MORE YEARS?

In late summer and early fall 2015 Donald Trump's campaign for the presidency was viewed as a long shot. A Gallup poll taken at the time of his announcement found that fully 75 percent of Americans did not consider him to be a serious candidate.[16] Political Scientist Larry Sabato described

Trump as an "early season fling for many people, fun while it lasts but doomed to breakup somewhere along the path to the nomination."[17] Political prognosticator Nate Silver told CNN's Andersen Cooper that Trump had maybe a 5 percent chance of becoming the Republican nominee.[18]

Forecasts for Trump winning the presidency were not much better in late summer and early fall 2016. In September, Obama's 2008 campaign manager David Plouffe said Clinton had a 100 percent chance of winning. Three weeks prior to the election, NPR's lead political editor Domenico Montanaro wrote, "Hillary Clinton is winning—and it's not close." Using a baseball analogy, he added, "Trump winning would be something like coming back from being down 3-0 in a best-of-seven baseball series."[19]

As fate would have it, two weeks after his analogy, the Chicago Cubs rallied from a 3–1 deficit to win the World Series against the Cleveland Indians. Prior to the start of game five of the series, Rob Arthur of Nate Silver's *FiveThirtyEight* site stated that Trump had a better chance of winning the presidency than the Cubs had of winning the series. The Cubs won and Donald Trump was elected president one week after that. On Election Day, the final prediction from *Huffington Post*'s 2016 Election Prediction gave Clinton a 98 percent chance of victory.[20] So much for certainty.

As detailed in chapter 4, political science models were far less certain of Trump's defeat in 2016. After all, two hundred years of historical precedent pointed to a Republican win. So where do things stand in early fall 2019? Trump's poll numbers in key battleground states are not great. His approval rating is underwater in most states, but most crucially in the battleground states of Michigan, Ohio, Pennsylvania, North Carolina, and Wisconsin. Trump campaign polls from spring 2019 leaked to the press showed that Trump was losing in those battleground states. Trump's national approval rating, as averaged by *FiveThirtyEight*, was 42.1 percent as of mid-August. It's never a good sign for an incumbent to be polling below 50 percent.

But not all the news is bad for Trump. Late summer poll averages put his job approval at 46–47 percent, at or near the highest level during his presidency. His approval rating for handling the economy was usually a bit over 50 percent and the economic picture continued to look reasonably good. Polls showed Trump in competitive races with his potential Democratic challengers. If impeachment problems dissipate, Trump may be a formidable candidate for reelection.

Though the numbers are not great for Trump, they weren't great in 2016 either. Most voters did not like Trump in 2016, including many who ultimately voted for him. Trump consistently trailed Clinton in national and battleground state polls, but still eked out a victory.

History is illustrative as well. In the past eleven presidential elections with incumbent candidates, the incumbents have won eight of the eleven. The only incumbent losers were Gerald Ford in 1976, Jimmy Carter in 1980, and George H. W. Bush in 1992. Ford was dogged by the Watergate scandal and his pardon of Nixon, while Carter and Bush were hobbled by weak economies. Even George W. Bush, who had lost the popular vote to Al Gore in 2000, secured reelection in 2004 despite an approval rating hovering near or below 50 percent at the time of the election.

So what to make of all of this? Will Trump join Ford, Carter, and Bush I or will he secure a second term? Making such a prediction about the 2020 result would be a fool's errand. That being said, Trump's odds of winning are strong enough to keep the vast majority of Congressional Republicans in his camp and to scare off any serious challenge for the nomination despite ongoing impeachment battles. His odds are weak enough to embolden Congressional Democrats to delay and obstruct his agenda while pursuing the types of investigations that distract and annoy the president. Continuity is often a safe bet in life and in politics.

SO, OVERALL . . .

For all the sound and fury of the Trump presidency, The Donald's time at 1600 Pennsylvania Avenue seems unlikely to reshape the three defining traits of our present political era. Recalling Byron Shafer's analysis,

Trump is the personification of an "era of political volatility" and his controversial persona seems likely to maintain a "long stretch of intense partisan warfare" during his presidency. Many of his reversals of Obama's unilateral executive actions can be quickly overturned by a rival successor in the White House. Trump's unpopularity and negative media coverage, however, may alter the "close partisan balance" that Shafer notes characterizes our political present, to the detriment of the Republican Party.

Rising economic inequality and the loss of manufacturing jobs have plagued the nation's economy for decades and it's unlikely that any Trump administration policies will reverse those trends in the short term—even if they pass Congress, which is far from certain. Popular discontent and low trust in government, festering since the 1960s, helped elect Trump. His ongoing criticisms of establishment Washington help to maintain that low trust and discontent. Foreign policy remains his greatest opportunity for a lasting legacy, for good or ill.

Donald Trump's highly unorthodox presidency features extraordinary levels of verbal swordplay, much generated by the president himself. The cumulative result of all the querulous verbiage may be remarkably modest. Consider this saying attributed to Mark Twain: "Action speaks louder than words but not nearly as often."

NOTES

CHAPTER 1. OUR ANGRY POLITICS

1. Frank. R. Baumgartner, Jeffrey M. Berry, Marie Hojnacki, David C. Kimball, and Beth L. Leech, "Money, Priorities, and Stalemate: How Lobbying Affects Public Policy," *Election Law Journal* 13(1) (2014): 194–209.

2. Steven E. Schier and Todd Eberly, *Polarized: The Rise of Ideology in American Politics* (New York: Rowman & Littlefield, 2014).

3. Lawrence C. Dodd and Bruce I. Oppenheimer, *Congress Reconsidered* (Washington, DC: CQ Press, 2012).

4. John R. Hibbing and Elizabeth Theiss-Morse, *Stealth Democracy: Americans' Beliefs about How Government Should Work* (London: Cambridge University Press, 2002), 33.

5. Jedediah Britton-Purdy, "Populism's Two Paths," *The Nation*, October 13, 2016, https://www.thenation.com/article/the-two-populisms/.

6. Brian Montopoli, "Tea Party Supporters: Who They Are and What They Believe," CBS News, December 14, 2012, https://www.cbsnews.com/news/tea-party-supporters-who-they-are-and-what-they-believe/.

7. Matthew Herper, "Some Say Occupy Wall Street Protesters Aimless; Facts Say Otherwise," *Forbes*, March 8, 2012, https://www.forbes.com/sites/matthewherper/2011/10/07/some-say-occupy-wall-street-protesters-aimless-facts-say-otherwise/#711fb625376a.

8. John F. Harris, "Ross Perot—The Father of Trump," *Politico*, July 9, 2019, https://www.politico.com/story/2019/07/09/ross-perot-the-father-of-trump-1404720.

9. German Lopez, "The Past Year of Research Has Made It Very Clear: Trump Won Because of Racial Resentment," Vox, December 15, 2017, https://www.vox.com/identities/2017/12/15/16781222/trump-racism-economic-anxiety-study.

CHAPTER 2. OUR TROUBLED PARTIES

1. Gallup, "Party Affiliation/Gallup Historical Trends—Gallup News," June 24, 2019, https://news.gallup.com/poll/15370/party-affiliation.aspx.

2. Daniel J. Coffey, "More Than a Dime's Worth: Using State Party Platforms to Assess the Degree of American Party Polarization," *PS: Political Science and Politics* 44(2) (2011): 331–37.

3. Steven Hill, "Divided We Stand: The Polarizing of American Politics." *National Civic Review* (Winter 2005): 3–14, 14.

4. See Pietro S. Nivola and David W. Brady, eds. Red and Blue Nation? *Characteristics and Causes of America's Polarized Politics.* Washington, DC: Brookings Institution Press, 2006.

5. Alan I. Abramowitz, *The Disappearing Center: Engaged Citizens, Polarization, and American Democracy.* New Haven, CT: Yale University Press, 2010.

6. Eric Groenendyk, "Competing Motives in a Polarized Electorate: Political Responsiveness, Identity Defensiveness, and the Rise of Partisan Antipathy," *Political Psychology* 39 (2018): 159–71.

7. Daniel Yudkin, Stephen Hawkins, and Tim Dixon, "The Perception Gap: How False Impressions Are Pulling Americans Apart," More in Common, 2019, https://perceptiongap.us/media/anvpqwr2/perception-gap-report-1-0-3.pdf.

8. Yudkin, Hawkins, and Dixon, "The Perception Gap."

9. Shanto Iyengar and Sean J. Westwood, "Fear and Loathing across Party Lines: New Evidence on Group Polarization," *American Journal of Political Science* 59(3) (2015): 690–707.

10. Groenendyk, "Competing Motives in a Polarized Electorate."

11. Stefan Wojcik and Adam Hughes, "How Twitter Users Compare to the General Public," Pew, April 24, 2019, https://www.pewinternet.org/2019/04/24/sizing-up-twitter-users/.

12. Carroll Doherty, Jocelyn Kiley and Bridget Johnson, "The Partisan Divide on Political Values Grows Even Wider," Pew, October 5, 2017, https://www.people-press.org/2017/10/05/8-partisan-animosity-personal-politics-views-of-trump/8_02/.

13. Naomi Jagoda, "Poll: 34 Percent Approve of Trump's Tax Law," *The Hill*, May 15, 2019, https://thehill.com/policy/finance/439275-poll-34-percent-approve-of-trumps-tax-law.

14. Groenendyk, "Competing Motives in a Polarized Electorate," 171.

15. Michael Kruse and Manu Raju, "Can Bernie Sanders Win the Love of a Party He Scorns?" *Politico*, August 10, 2015, https://www.politico.com/magazine/story/2015/08/bernie-sanders-2016-democrats-121181.

16. Tom Murse, "Was Donald Trump Really a Democrat?" ThoughtCo, May 25, 2019, https://www.thoughtco.com/was-donald-trump-a-democrat-3367571.

17. Rory Carrol, "Hillary Clinton: Trump Is Too Dangerous and Unstable to Have the Nuclear Codes," *The Guardian*, June 2, 2016, https://www.theguardian.com/us-news/2016/jun/02/hillary-clinton-donald-trump-speech-foreign-policy-security.

18. Philip Bump, "4.4 Million 2012 Obama Voters Stayed Home in 2016," *Washington Post*, March 12, 2018, https://www.washingtonpost.com/news/politics/wp/2018/03/12/4-4-million-2012-obama-voters-stayed-home-in-2016-more-than-a-third-of-them-black/.

19. Christina Wilkie, "A 'Kavanaugh Bump' Is Boosting GOP Senate Candidates—But Its Impact on Trump's Ratings Is Unclear," CNBC, October 13, 2018, https://www.cnbc.com/2018/10/13/kavanaugh-bump-is-boosting-gop-senate-candidates-but-trump-is-a-different-story.html.

20. The Avalon Project, "Washington's Farewell Address 1796," Yale Law School. https://avalon.law.yale.edu/18th_century/washing.asp.

CHAPTER 3. TRUMP THE CELEBRITY

1. Neal Gabler, *Toward a New Definition of Celebrity* (Los Angeles: The Norman Lear Center, 2001), 4.

2. Mark Harvey, *Celebrity Influence: Politics, Persuasion and Issue-Based Advocacy* (Lawrence: University Press of Kansas, 2017), 3.

3. Harvey, *Celebrity Influence*, 112–16.

4. This chapter's story of Trump's life and career derives from widely reported information in a variety of books. This chapter's account employs several works in relating that tale. An impressively detailed biography is Michael Kranish and Marc Fisher, *Trump Revealed: The Definitive Biography of the 45th President* (New York: Scribner, 2016). Trump's celebrity career receives thorough treatment in Robert Slater, *No Such Thing as Over-Exposure: Inside the Life and Celebrity of Donald Trump* (Upper Saddle River, NJ: Pearson Prentice Hall, 2005). Other useful sources include Timothy L. O'Brien, *Trump Nation: The Art of Being the Donald* (New York: Grand Central Publishing, 2016); David Cay Johnson, *The Making of Donald Trump* (Brooklyn: Melville House, 2016); Corey R. Lewandowski and David N. Bossie, *Let Trump Be Trump: The Inside Story of His Rise to the Presidency* (New York: Center Street, 2017); Donald J. Trump with Tony Schwartz, *Trump: The Art of the Deal* (New York: Ballantine Books, 2015); and Donald J. Trump and Bill Zanker, *Think Big: Make It Happen in Business and Life* (New York: HarperCollins, 2007).

5. Slater, *Over-Exposure*, 48.

6. Trump and Zanker, *Think Big*, 151.

7. The account in this section derives from Jane Mayer, "Donald Trump's Ghostwriter Tells All," *New Yorker*, July 25, 2016, https://www.newyorker.com/magazine/2016/07/25/donald-trumps-ghostwriter-tells-all.

8. Trump, *Art of the Deal*, 57–58.

9. Kranish and Fisher, *Trump Revealed*, 204.

10. Quoted in Slater, *Over-Exposure*, 109.

11. Quoted in Kranish and Fisher, *Trump Revealed*, 215.

12. Trump and Zanker, *Think Big*, 190 and 139.

13. W. Rhys Roberts, trans., *Rhetorica: The Works of Aristotle*, Vol. 11 (Oxford: Clarendon Press, 1924). Reprint 1954 in Aristotle, *Rhetoric and Poetics* (translated by Roberts and Ingram Bywater) (New York: Modern Library), 141.

14. David Lynn Painter and Katherine Rizzo, "The Verbal Tone of the 2016 Presidential Primaries: Candidate Twitter, Debate, and Campaign Speech Rhetoric," in *The Presidency and Social Media*, eds. Dan Schill and John Allen Hendricks (New York: Routledge, 2018), 155.

CHAPTER 4. TRUMP'S 2016 BREAKTHROUGHS

1. Peter L. Francia, "Free Media and Twitter in the 2016 Presidential Election: The Unconventional Campaign of Donald Trump," *Social Science Computer Review* 30(10) (2017): 7–8. Campaign spending totals in this paragraph are from Francia's analysis.

2. Stephen Reicher and S. Alexander Haslam, "The Politics of Hope: Donald Trump as an Entrepreneur of Identity," in *Why Irrational Politics Appeals: Understanding the Allure of Trump*, ed. Mari Fitzduff (Santa Barbara, CA: Praeger, 2017), 29.

3. "Even the Firm That Hired Actors to Cheer Trump's Campaign Launch Had to Wait to Be Paid," *Washington Post*, June 12, 2019, https://www.washingtonpost.com/news/the-fix/wp/2017/01/20/even-the-firm-that-hired-actors-to-cheer-trumps-campaign-launch-had-to-wait-to-be-paid/.

4. "Donald Trump's Tirade on Mexico's 'Drugs and Rapists' Outrages US Latinos," *The Guardian*, June 12, 2019, https://www.theguardian.com/us-news/2015/jun/16/donald-trump-mexico-presidential-speech-latino-hispanic.

5. "Donald Trump's Presidential Announcement Speech," *Time*, June 16, 2015, https://time.com/3923128/donald-trump-announcement-speech/.

6. Sam Levine, "Donald Trump on John McCain's War Record: 'I Like People Who Weren't Captured.'" *Huffington Post*, July 18, 2015, https://www.huffpost.com/entry/donald-trump-john-mccain_n_55aa7ff1e4b0caf721b2feb7.

7. David A. Fahrenthold, "Trump Recorded Having Extremely Lewd Conversation about Women in 2005," *Washington Post*, October 8, 2015, https://www.washingtonpost.com/politics/trump-recorded-having-extremely-lewd-conversation-about-women-in-2005/2016/10/07/3b9ce776-8cb4-11e6-bf8a-3d26847eeed4_story.html.

8. Thomas E. Patterson, "News Coverage of Donald Trump's First 100 Days," Shorenstein Center, May 18, 2017, https://shorensteincenter.org/news-coverage-donald-trumps-first-100-days/.

9. Patterson, "News Coverage of Donald Trump's First 100 Days."

10. Patterson, "News Coverage of Donald Trump's First 100 Days."

11. Nicholas Kristof, "My Shared Shame: The Media Helped Make Trump," *New York Times*, March 26, 2016, https://www.nytimes.com/2016/03/27/opinion/sunday/my-shared-shame-the-media-helped-make-trump.html?_r=0.

12. Patterson, "News Coverage of Donald Trump's First 100 Days."

13. "Trump Tops Republican Pack by Wide Margin, Quinnipiac University National Poll Finds; But Dems Trump Trump in General Election," Quinnipiac Poll, July 30, 2015, https://poll.qu.edu/national/release-detail?ReleaseID=2264.

14. Patterson, "News Coverage of Donald Trump's First 100 Days."

15. Patterson, "News Coverage of Donald Trump's First 100 Days."

16. Sean Sullivan, "Trump Brings Complaints of 'Rigged,' 'Phony' Nominating Process to Indiana Debut," *Washington Post*, April 20, 2016, https://www.washingtonpost.com/news/post-politics/wp/2016/04/20/trump-brings-complaints-of-rigged-phony-nominating-process-to-indiana-debut/.

17. Jonathan Chait, "Sanders Says 2016 Was Rigged, Won't Pledge to Support Winner," *New York Magazine*, June 26, 2019, http://nymag.com/intelligencer/2019/06/bernie-sanders-2016-rigged-wont-pledge-support-winner.html.

18. Eli Skokols, "Why Trump Says It's All 'Rigged,'" *Politico*, August 2, 2016, https://www.politico.com/story/2016/08/donald-trump-rigged-election-226588.

19. Jennifer Sclafani, *Talking Donald Trump: A Sociolinguistic Study of Style, Metadiscourse, and Political Identity* (New York: Routledge, 2017).

20. "Transcript: President Trump's Exchange with CNN's Jim Acosta," CNN, February 20, 2016, https://money.cnn.com/2017/02/16/media/jim-acosta-donald-trump-press-conference/.

21. Danielle Kurtzleben, "Pollsters Find 'At Best Mixed Evidence' Comey Letter Swayed Election," NPR, May 5, 2017, http://www.npr.org/2017/05/05/526936636/pollsters-find-at-best-mixed-evidence-comey-letter-swayed-election.

22. Christopher J. Devine and Kyle C. Kopko, "5 Things You Need to Know about How Third-Party Candidates Did in 2016," *Washington Post*, November 15, 2016, https://www.washingtonpost.com/news/monkey-cage/wp/2016/11/15/5-things-you-need-to-know-about-how-third-party-candidates-did-in-2016/?noredirect=on.

23. John B. Judis and Ruy Teixeira, *The Emerging Democratic Majority* (New York: Simon and Schuster, 2002).

24. Harry Enten, "Registered Voters Who Stayed Home Probably Cost Clinton the Election," *FiveThirtyEight*, January 5, 2017, https://fivethirtyeight.com/features/registered-voters-who-stayed-home-probably-cost-clinton-the-election/.

25. Sean Trende and David Byler, "How Trump Won—Conclusions," RealClearPolitics, January 5, 2017, https://www.realclearpolitics.com/articles/2017/01/20/how_trump_won_—_conclusions_132846.html.

26. Trende and Byler, "How Trump Won—Conclusions."

27. Dan McLaughlin, "The Real Reason Trump Won," *National Review*, January 10, 2017, https://www.nationalreview.com/2017/01/barack-obama-real-reason-trump-won/.

CHAPTER 5. PRESIDENT TRUMP

1. Clinton Rossiter, "The Presidency—Focus of Leadership," *New York Times*, November 11, 1956, https://www.nytimes.com/1956/11/11/archives/the-presidency-focus-of-leadership-as-our-one-truly-national.html.

2. Steven J. Rubenzer and Thomas R. Faschingbauer, *Personality, Character and Leadership in the White House: Psychologists Assess the Presidents* (Washington, DC: Brassey's, 2004), 83.

3. Peter Jacobs, "John Bolton Reportedly Promised Trump He Wouldn't 'Start Any Wars' as National Security Advisor," *Business Insider*, March 23, 2018, https://www.businessinsider.in/john-bolton-reportedly-promised-trump-he-wouldnt-start-any-wars-as-national-security-adviser/articleshow/63422155.cms.

4. Kathryn Dun Tenpas, "Tracking Turnover in the Trump Administration," Brookings, August 2019, https://www.brookings.edu/research/tracking-turnover-in-the-trump-administration/.

5. Ashley Parker, "Snubs and Slights Are Part of the Job in Trump's White House," *Washington Post*, May 29, 2017, https://www.washingtonpost.com/politics/snubs-and-slights-are-part-of-the-job-in-trumps-white-house/2017/05/29/f5c9d5c0-417a-11e7-9869-bac8b446820a_story.html?utm term=.3c7461aee973.

6. Marshall Frady, "The Big Guy," *New York Review of Books*, November 1, 2002, http://www.nybooks.com/articles/2002/11/07/the-big-guy/.

7. "Redacted Mueller Report," *Politico*, April 18, 2019, p. 10, https://www.politico.com/story/2019/04/18/mueller-report-pdf-download-text-file-1280891.

8. Eliza Relman, "Attorney General Says Trump Fully Cooperated with Mueller Investigation, but He Didn't Sit for an Interview," *Business Insider*,

April 18, 2019, https://www.businessinsider.com/barr-says-trump-fully-coop
erated-mueller-investigation-2019-4.

9. Randall Lane, "Trump Unfiltered: The Full Transcript of the President's
Interview with *Forbes*," *Forbes*, October 10, 2017, https://www.forbes.com/
sites/randalllane/2017/10/10/trump-unfiltered/#6125fb917a58.

CHAPTER 6. THE TRUMP AGENDA

1. Ryan Teague Beckwith, "Read Donald Trump's 'America First' Foreign
Policy Speech," *Time*, April 27, 2016, http://time.com/4309786/read-donald
-trumps-america-first-foreign-policy-speech/?xid=time_socialflow_twitter.

2. Kristin Huang, "Five Trade Issues the US and China Need to Tackle
before Trump Goes to Beijing," *South China Morning Post*, September 26,
2017, https://www.scmp.com/news/china/diplomacy-defence/article/2112872/
stumbling-blocks-america-and-china-must-overcome.

3. Luiza Ch. Savage and John F. Harris, "Trump's Method to the Madness
on Trade," *Politico*, June 6, 2019, https://www.politico.com/story/2019/06/06/
donald-trump-trade-policy-global-translations-1355868.

4. Ali Vitali, "Trump on North Korea Feud: 'Fire and Fury' Not Tough
Enough," NBC News, August 10, 2017, http://www.nbcnews.com/politics/
white-house/trump-north-korea-feud-fire-fury-not-tough-enough-n791561.

CHAPTER 7. TRUMP'S FUTURE

1. Steven E. Schier and Todd E. Eberly, *American Government and Popular
Discontent: Stability without Success* (New York: Routledge, 2013), 29.

2. Drew Desilver, "The Many Ways to Measure Economic Inequality,"
Pew Research Center, September 22, 2015, http://www.pewresearch.org/fact
-tank/2015/09/22/the-many-ways-to-measure-economic-inequality/.

3. Tami Luhby, "The Middle Class Gets a Big Raise . . . Finally," CNN
Money, September 13, 2016, http://money.cnn.com/2016/09/13/news/econ
omy/median-income-census/index.html.

4. Richard Fry and Rakesh Kochhar, "America's Wealth Gap between
Middle-Income and Upper-Income Families Is Widest on Record," Pew

Research Center, December 17, 2014, http://www.pewresearch.org/fact
-tank/2014/12/17/wealth-gap-upper-middle-income/.

5. Luhby, "The Middle Class Gets a Big Raise . . . Finally."

6. Federal Reserve Board, "Survey of Consumer Finances," July 11, 2013,
https://www.federalreserve.gov/econres/scfindex.htm.

7. Bureau of Labor Statistics, "Table B-1: Employees on Nonfarm Pay-
rolls," February 5, 2017, https://www.bls.gov/webapps/legacy/cesbtab1.htm.

8. Edward Alden, *Failure to Adjust: How Americans Got Left behind the
Global Economy* (Lanham, MD: Rowman & Littlefield, 2017). The two quotations are from pages 5 and 17, respectively.

9. Schier and Eberly, *American Government and Popular Discontent*, 29–30.

10. Byron E. Shafer, *The American Political Pattern* (Lawrence: University
Press of Kansas, 2016). The quotations are from pages 123, 191, and 167,
respectively.

11. Pew Research Center, "Public Has Criticisms of Both Parties, but Democrats Lead on Empathy for Middle Class," June 20, 2017, http://www.people
-press.org/2017/06/20/public-has-criticisms-of-both-parties-but-democrats
-lead-on-empathy-for-middle-class/.

12. Jeffrey M. Jones, "Republican Favorability Down; Views of Democrats
Steady," Gallup.com, January 9, 2019, https://news.gallup.com/poll/246341/
republican-favorability-down-views-democrats-steady.aspx.

13. John T. Bennett, "Trump's Winning Pattern with Legislation Might
Become a Thing of the Past: CQ Vote Studies," Roll Call, February 28, 2019,
https://www.rollcall.com/news/congress/trump-vote-study-legislation.

14. Schier and Eberly, *American Government and Popular Discontent*, 95.

15. Stephen Skowronek, *The Politics Presidents Make: Leadership from
John Adams to Bill Clinton* (Cambridge, MA: Harvard University Press,
1997), 449.

16. Briony Swire, Adam J. Berinsky, Stephan Lewandowsky, and Ullrich K.
H. Ecker, "Processing Political Information: Comprehending the Trump Phenomenon," *Royal Society Open Science* (4)3 (2017), https://royalsocietypublish
ing.org/doi/10.1098/rsos.160802.

17. Larry J. Sabato's Crystal Ball, "Republicans 2016: What to Do with
The Donald?" August 13, 2015, http://www.centerforpolitics.org/crystalball/
articles/republicans-2016-what-to-do-with-the-donald/.

18. Nate Silver, "Trump Has about 5% Chance of Winning," RealClearPolitics September 15, 2015, https://www.realclearpolitics.com/video/2015/09/15/nate_silver_trump_has_about_5_chance_of_winning.html.

19. "Battleground Map: Hillary Clinton Is Winning—And It's Not Close," National Public Radio, October 18, 2016, https://www.npr.org/2016/10/18/498406765/npr-battleground-map-hillary-clinton-is-winning-and-its-not-close.

20. "2016 President Forecast," *Huffington Post*, October 3, 2016, https://elections.huffingtonpost.com/2016/forecast/president.

INDEX

tax reform, 11, 32, 87, 113, 123

tax returns controversy, 98–99

Tea Party movement, 11, 12, 35, 63, 80

Teixeira, Ruy, 81–83, 84

Think Big (Trump, D. J., and Zanker), 60

Tillerson, Rex, 92, 120

trade, international, 35, 135; with China, 72, 89, 116–17; Trump, D. J., campaign (2016) on, 17, 72, 87, 116; Trump, D. J., presidency on, 116–18, 123, 127

Treasury Department/Secretary, 5, 92

Trende, Sean, 83

Trump, Barron (son), 58

Trump, D. J., campaign (2016): on Affordable Care Act, 37, 72, 107; announcement speech for, 33, 71–72, 107; Bush, J., campaign contrasted with, 74–76; celebrity career role in success of, 17, 18, 63–65, 70–71, 72–73; Clinton, H., attacks by, 37, 40; communication style role in, 78; controversies in, 73–74, 77; on foreign policy, 87, 116; Fox News role in, 64; funding for, 68; GOP nomination issues and, 77; hyperbole used in, 64, 78; on immigration, 14, 61, 72; media exposure role in, 68, 71–78; on Mexican immigration, 61, 72; on Mexico border wall, 69, 87; Muslim ban proposed in, 74; Obama attacks in, 40, 63, 116;

opponent insult approach in, 69–70; polls and opinion about, 138–39; popular discontent channeled in, 16, 36, 129; populism rhetoric of, 13, 14, 35–37; promises made under, 72, 87–88, 107; rallies, 14, 68–69; on rigged system, 77; social media use, 17, 67, 69–70, 73, 74; staff and management, 67–68; symbols and slogans in, 46, 67, 70–71, 116; tactics, 18; Tea Party movement relation to, 12, 35, 80; on trade policies, 72, 87, 107, 116

Trump, D. J., presidency: Affordable Care Act repeal under, 32; appointments and turnover in, 90–95, 104, 130, 134–35; approval surveys, 130–31, 139–40; cabinet appointments and turnover under, 90–95, 104, 130; celebrity career compared with approach to, 44; celebrity politics era with, 19; China trade negotiations under, 116–17; deregulation and Obama policies rollback under, 107–11; "dominator" style of, 88–89, 97, 104; economic growth under, 128; environmental and energy policy under, 107–8, 109–10, 122, 138; ethics issues under, 97–100; on fake news, 124; false statements made under, 89; federal judiciary restructuring under, 38–39, 114–15; fiscal

ABOUT THE AUTHORS

Steven E. Schier is Dorothy H. and Edward C. Congdon Professor Emeritus of Political Science at Carleton College, where he taught for thirty-six years. Twelve times he directed the Carleton in Washington program, an off-campus term of study he founded in 1983. Dr. Schier is the author, co-author, or editor of twenty-two books. His most recent titles for Rowman & Littlefield are *The Trump Presidency: Outsider in the Oval Office* (2017), coauthored with Todd E. Eberly; *Debating the Obama Presidency* (2016), an edited volume; and *Polarized: The Rise of Ideology in US Politics* (2016), also coauthored with Todd E. Eberly.

Todd E. Eberly is professor of political science and public policy at St. Mary's College of Maryland. He specializes in contemporary American politics with a focus on the effect of polarization on voters, government, and governing. Professor Eberly has written four books with Steven Schier of Carleton College. Their first book, *American Government and Popular Discontent* was released in June 2013. Their second book, *The Rise of Ideology in America*, was released in 2015. Their third book, *The Trump Presidency: Outsider in the Oval Office* was published in September 2017. Professor Eberly is an advisor to Project Vote Smart and his analysis and commentary have been featured in the *Washington Post*, the *Baltimore Sun*, CNBC, and public radio/television. He has served as an expert witness in cases challenging gerrymandered congressional districts and has consulted with the centrist organization Third Way. He was named one of the most influential voices in Maryland politics by *Campaigns and Elections* magazine and the St. Mary's College Student Government Association honored him with the Faculty Student Life Award. He lives in Southern, Maryland, with his wife and two daughters.